Be It Until You Become It

Advance Praise for
Be It Until You Become It

"Natasha Graziano came into my life as a miracle. And it is as if she planted a garden of Miracles that bloomed in the past two years. Natasha, her MBS method, and her overwhelming generosity of spirit have been integral in a monumental shift in my life toward profound physical and emotional healing.

When I first met Natasha, I was struggling with crippling nerve pain and weakness from a car accident that left me with several fractured vertebrae and multiple muscle tears as well as a fractured relationship. After initial recovery, my career was catapulting. However, I struggled to keep up under the strain of chronic pain and grief at the loss of what I thought was a lifetime love.

Through personal mentoring and group sessions, Natasha gave me the tools to shift my life from recovery to revelation to living a real-life dream. Action Plan and Action Steps with Real Results. She leads with Compassion by Example"

—**Mela Lee,** Voice Actress
(Disney/ Marvel/ Apex Legends)

"Natasha has written a powerful book which is a compelling intertwine of neuroscience and ancient wisdom. It is ideal for anyone wanting to create abundance in any area of their life. Her methods are very tangible and can be applied by anyone to live a happier, more fulfilling life and become the person they want to be."

—**John Assaraf,** author of bestselling book *The Secret*, CEO of Neurogym, *New York Times* bestselling author

"If you're feeling stuck or exhausted or you're ready to reinvent yourself, but you're not sure where to begin, this is the book for you! *Be It Until You Become It* is a powerful step-by-step guide to transforming your life. Natasha's story of her journey from victim to victor will leave you feeling motivated and inspired, while her MBS Method will help you overcome the blocks that are holding you back from becoming the best version of you!"

— **Jenna Kutcher,** bestselling author and host of *The Goal Digger* podcast

"Natasha is the epitome of growth! Her mindset and belief in herself to become whoever and whatever she wants is beyond frikin inspiring! If you are looking to change your life and believe it's possible then Natasha is the perfect guide and cheerleader to take with you on that journey."

— **Lisa Bilyeu,** host of *Women Of Impact* podcast and bestselling author

"Natasha's way of writing will resonate with people that really need help. Every person needs to read *Be It Until You Become It.*"

— **Chris Branch,** Oscar Award Winning Film Producer

"An incredible book, with a stunning author who's decided to give her life over to others who are down and out. *Be It Until You Become It* has helped me and I know it will help you! Natasha is literally a modern day Gandhi!"

— **Gigi Gorgeous Getty,** Internet sensation, Transgender icon, Author, Model, Actress.

"Simply mind blowing. A book filled with practices and advice that will change your life. It's changed mine."

— **NATS GETTY,** Designer, Activist, Philanthropist, Artist

BE IT UNTIL YOU BECOME IT

The Law of Attraction Explained Through Neuroscience and Ancient Wisdom

Named #1 Female Mindset Coach
Natasha Graziano

NEW YORK

LONDON • NASHVILLE • MELBOURNE • VANCOUVER

Be It Until You Become It

The Law of Attraction Explained Through Neuroscience and Ancient Wisdom

Published in New York, New York, by Morgan James Publishing. Morgan James is a trademark of Morgan James, LLC. www.MorganJamesPublishing.com

Proudly distributed by Ingram Publisher Services.

Scriptures taken from the Holy Bible, New International Version®, NIV®. Copyright © 1973, 1978, 1984, 2011 by Biblica, Inc.™ Used by permission of Zondervan. All rights reserved worldwide. www.zondervan.com The "NIV" and "New International Version" are trademarks registered in the United States Patent and Trademark Office by Biblica, Inc.™

Morgan James BOGO™

A **FREE** ebook edition is available for you or a friend with the purchase of this print book.

CLEARLY SIGN YOUR NAME ABOVE

Instructions to claim your free ebook edition:
1. Visit MorganJamesBOGO.com
2. Sign your name CLEARLY in the space above
3. Complete the form and submit a photo of this entire page
4. You or your friend can download the ebook to your preferred device

ISBN 9781631959295 paperback
ISBN 9781631959301 ebook
Library of Congress Control Number: 2022935293

Cover Design by:
Camila Cuéllar Bejarano

Interior Design by:
Christopher Kirk
www.GFSstudio.com

Cover Photo by:
Mark X Photos

Author Photo by:
Elizabeth Hook

Morgan James is a proud partner of Habitat for Humanity Peninsula and Greater Williamsburg. Partners in building since 2006.

Get involved today! Visit MorganJamesPublishing.com/giving-back

Download Your Free Gifts!

Photograph by Elizabeth Hook

Before you start reading . . .

*I wanted to say, from the bottom of my heart, how grateful
I am that you have bought this book. I don't take a single
reader for granted, and I know that this book has the answer
that you need to change your life right now.
On that note, I wanted to offer you a bonus gift to accompany
your read. It is FREE just for my readers!*

*To download your FREE gift, visit:
www.NatashaGraziano.com/Freegift
Or use the QR code below to take you directly there!*

Free Gift

This book is dedicated to you, the reader.
You are, with the power of the Universe behind you, the
co-creator of your reality, attracting new possibilities,
people, circumstances, and places to you like a magnet.

I'd also like to dedicate this book to my son, Rio. Thank you for
inspiring me to rise up and be a role model and mother to you,
even through my darkest moments. Because of you, I have this
mission to help humanity unlock and reach their full potential.

The future is not yet written, it is in your hands . . .

Table of Contents

How I Found the Missing Secret to the Law of Attraction

In 2017, I endured the worst year of my life. My entire world came crumbling down around me. I found myself bedridden with an illness, and my mind was consumed by chronic anxiety. Rewind even further to 2013. I had experienced traumatic sexual abuse and developed an unsustainable drug addiction that led me to become a webcam girl to feed my lifestyle and addiction. My body was exploited to the point that I had lost myself completely. The truth is that I honestly don't remember half the things I did back then because I was high most of the time. It was those poor decisions that eventually landed me as a broke, homeless single mom.

After losing all the money I had to my name and finding myself without a home, I realized that I wasn't listening to what the Universe was trying to tell me. When you lose everything and are financially, emotionally, spiritually, mentally, and physically broken, the only place left to look for answers is inward. There was nothing left on the outside worth seeing anymore. It was all gone.

But it was from those dark depths of pain and suffering that I found my purpose.

I knew if I could just learn how to press the reset button and bounce back using everything I had learned, I would bring myself back to what I call "full sparkle." I would be more empowered than ever before.

I had an important message for the world. I wanted to make my knowledge about healing and manifesting go viral so that every single person on the planet could know that they too could rise far beyond the limiting mental constructs that hold millions of people back from achieving their true purpose—whether that purpose be wealth, health, happiness, success, or love. And lo and behold, my new life mission was born. I would stop at nothing to make myself heard. I had learned that the secret to manifesting the life of my dreams was to first be the version of me I wanted to become through my mind, body, and habits—then I would become her.

That secret first came to me when I was standing in front of the mirror after a long flight. Quite honestly, it was a miracle I'd made it there in the first place. I was taking strong heart medication at that time, and the health risks were through the roof, not to mention I was deeply depressed. I remember staring at my reflection in the mirror of the hotel bathroom, bawling from both physical and emotional pain. I was ready to leave this world. Tears ran down my face, and I could barely breathe. I couldn't hold my tears back anymore. I knew I desperately needed something to help me cope, to help me deal with the tsunami of emotions dominating my inner reality. It was at that very moment I knew I couldn't do what I was doing anymore. I had to find a cure. In fact, I knew I had to turn my adversity into my cure. And as I surrendered to that moment, I saw a flicker of light in my mind.

My first impulse was to search for motivational videos online. I stumbled upon the motivational tracks of Denzel Washington and immediately started listening to them on repeat over and over until his words started to permeate my soul. As they did, I slowly got closer to my reflection in the mirror, until I found myself literally pressed against it. Staring deeply and directly into my own eyes, I saw my soul for the first time.

When you look into your eyes through your reflection, the depths of your soul reveal themselves; the immensity of your whole being, all your strengths and weaknesses, is suddenly recognized. With tears still streaming down my face, I began preaching words of encouragement and hope back into my soul, relighting a fire back into my very essence. Charged with a force beyond my knowing, I started speaking powerfully at my own reflection: "You are healed. This is only temporary. What you're going through now is not you, and it's not who you're meant to be. This is not your destiny. You *are* meant for more. You were born into this world to achieve greatness, to help others. Don't dim your light now; shine brighter."

That glimmer of light I felt when I first surrendered began glowing and shining like a compass, pointing me to my purpose. I realized that every single day, no matter what you're going through, you will always see a glimmer of light like a candle. And if you focus on that light, you can follow it out of the darkness. This is the light that can guide you to long-lasting happiness.

I channeled that message, suddenly understanding that the Universe would always give me a light to guide my way. Powerful energies merged with my being, and I received the most powerful message of all. Speaking with such clarity and directness that the words seemed to soar through me, I declared, "You're going to be a motivational speaker and coach other people."

Even as I said those words, I couldn't help but think, "Me? A public speaker? A mindset coach? I can barely even talk to people; how could I ever speak on stage?" But I'd gotten the message loud and clear. I wouldn't understand the reason until much later.

When I think about that moment now, it actually blows my mind, because only a few years later, I'm speaking on the biggest stages in the world alongside inspiring, influential humans. I've shared stages both in person and online with the likes of Tony Robbins, Marc Randolph (the co-founder of Netflix), Jesse Itzler, Jim Kwik, Dan Fleyshman, Mark Cuban,

How I Found the Missing Secret to the Law of Attraction | xvii

Daymond John, and some of the co-authors who wrote one of my all-time favorite books, *The Secret*, to name a few. I've even collaborated with some of these great coaches, aligning our missions to create an even more profound impact on the world together.

When you look back on anything that has happened in your life, you always see the light, the lesson, and the reason behind the challenges you had to endure. Even though, at times, those challenges may have been painful, hindsight reveals how each experience helps us take another step on our soul's journey, guiding us to where we are now and the person we are today.

Listening to Denzel Washington's words, preaching to my own reflection, embedding new affirmative beliefs, I felt the light of realization pour over me. It didn't matter that some of the words I was saying over myself weren't true at the time. All that mattered was that I made myself believe them.

| *My breakdown was becoming my breakthrough.* |

And this truly is the secret behind *Be It Until You Become It*: being the version of yourself you wish to be before you become them. I dive into this in great detail through this book with a five-step process combining neuroscience, ancient wisdom, and my world-renowned Meditational Behavioral Synchronicity (MBS) method. It was in my darkest hour that I knew I had found the missing secret to the law of attraction—

the secret I will be sharing with you throughout the pages of the very book in your hands right now.

From that moment on, it was clear to me that we all hold a limitless potential to have, be, and do *anything* we desire. We simply must believe in our own creative power, learn the tools to cultivate it, and believe that anything and everything is possible. I deserved a second chance. We all deserve a second chance. I understood what I had done wrong, where I had failed others and myself, and I decided it was my duty to help other people avoid making my same mistakes. I realized it was the moment to be who I deserved to be until I became her.

During my healing, my "rebirth" if you will, I would spend hours every day exploring different practices like meditation, breathwork, and even cold exposure. (I wrote about the power of these practices and your ability to create your best life in my first book, *The Action Plan*.) Throughout that year of suffering, awakening, and healing, it became clear there was no time to play the waiting game. I didn't want to wait years to be fully healed and regain the money I'd lost so that I could provide my son and I with even a basic quality of life. Essentially, I needed a miracle, and I needed it fast. I didn't want to just come back as an average girl; I wanted to come back stronger and more powerful than ever—and show others how to do so too.

My life truly transformed when I began to combine ancient practices spanning back thousands of years with modern neuroscience, something a mere fifty years ago wouldn't have been possible without the immense technological advancements of the last half a century. *That* was when my life truly changed. I remember the feeling so vividly. It was like I could breathe again, like a weight had been lifted, a burden off-loaded. I never dreamed this method I'd uncovered and developed would go on to serve so many people across the globe. It didn't occur to me that it could be just as powerful for another person as it was for me, and I'm humbled every day to know so many people have transformed their lives using this method.

In a very small space of time, I went from being broke to making my first million. I went from sick to vibrant, from lost to focused and motivated, from depressed to confident, from a single mom to marrying my soul mate, from homeless and living in my mom's basement with my son to living in my dream homes around the world. It's staggering to look back on everything I went through and acknowledge the present. They are two completely opposing experiences, but everything is part of my story and brought me to where I find myself now. And I am sure that without those painful lessons, I wouldn't be where I am today. I share my story and how I managed to become the person I am now so that you can learn from my mistakes and discover how you too can live your best life filled with happiness and abundance.

So, what was the missing secret for this huge transformation? I call it the *Meditational Behavioral Synchronic-*

ity (MBS) method. I'll be sharing more about that method throughout the pages of this book, so you too can apply this secret and unlock the door to anything you desire. The method combines powerful techniques, practices, and tools to unlock your potential and uplevel your life, as I did. The MBS method has been called three years of therapy in fifteen minutes. Later in this book, I dive deeper into the principles and roots of the MBS method.

If you're reading this, perhaps you're craving more from your life. Maybe you're feeling stuck as I once did, or perhaps you're enduring intolerable adversities or traumas you haven't yet released, longing for a breakthrough. Perhaps you have an awareness of your inner fire and want to ignite it and become the new, happier, more successful version of you. Well, I'm here as your personal cheerleader. Know that I believe in you. If I could do it, you can too!

When you embody the wisdom and apply the techniques in this book, the new road you're heading toward is one of ultimate success, optimal health, millions of dollars, abundance in every area of your life, a vision of happiness, bliss, confidence, and access to anything you could possibly desire—because this is the ultimate truth. Poverty, scarcity, lack, illness . . . these things may appear to exist in the physical realm; however, once you learn to tap into the limitless power of your mind, once you align your heart, mind, and soul to become one, your eyes will open to the only thing that really exists— abundance. The vibrational frequency of love will radiate from you, the vision you want to manifest will inundate your attention, materializing as your new reality.

Or, as Oprah Winfrey says, "You have to be it and radiate it and then it becomes you."

Chapter 1:

The Unlimited Power of the Subconscious Mind

The subconscious mind is where 98 percent of your thoughts and actions flow. If I were to ask what you truly want, what would you say? Would you know exactly what it is you are living for? Or would your mind be filled with all the material "stuff" you desire?

When people think about attracting wealth and abundance, their focus is usually external. The common belief is that you have to work really hard, graft your way to a high paid job, toiling all hours to achieve results, eventually collapsing from the exhaustion of the whole process. But what a lot of us fail to recognize is that the job of attracting abundance, wealth, or just about anything else you can imagine falls not on the act of generating anything external but predominantly depends on our mindset coupled with our relationship to money and our openness to receiving it. Any belief is simply a narrative we've *chosen* to believe and *identify* with. This is important because the potential power of our beliefs is enormously underrated. Luckily, our beliefs are something we can shift to align with our desires once we learn how to harness them under our conscious control. Attracting abundance is like holding the key that unlocks a door to limitless flow. Once you have the key—and gain control of your subconscious mind—you can have, be, and do anything you desire. The Universe will always say "yes" to you.

The subconscious mind is the part of the mind that acts on autopilot. Not directly within our focal awareness, it's a compilation of the skills, knowledge, and truths we've learned over the course of our lives. Though primarily acting unconsciously, it's largely responsible for our instinctive responses, gut feelings, thoughts (95 percent to be precise), and habits we implement every day without even noticing. These seemingly automatic habits might appear impossible to change. Perhaps you think they are just "who you are" or that it's "just the way things are"—sound familiar? Well, I'm here to tell you that once you learn how to access your subconscious mind, you'll soon realize that you hold immense power to shift your reality toward anything you desire. You can be abundant and wealthy in every area of your life. Berkeley author Luc LaMontagne explains that "certain conscious activities can help unveil the subconscious mind, in the same way that a painting provides insight about the paint, or in the way that an entreé provides insight about the ingredients, while the artist or chef is the conscious mind." What LaMontagne means is that by practicing activities consciously and consistently, you can easily "reconstruct the subconscious mind."[1]

The limiting beliefs about money that our society, schooling, and even parents have laid on us since we were young may have made you think that there's not enough for everyone or that God will love you more if you're humble. We've learned to believe that money is hard to get and hard to keep, that it doesn't grow on trees, and that it's only reserved for a lucky few.

Perhaps these beliefs sound painfully familiar; perhaps they've been impressed into your subconscious mind the same way they were in mine.

The source of a scarcity mentality is the environment we were raised in and the people within it. This isn't anyone's fault, of course; they're all doing the very best they can. What they ended up regurgitating to us is merely a reflection of their relationship with money; they didn't know any better! So, some end up living a life in which money flows easily and freely, and others, regardless of their level of wealth, lose it, waste it, save it obsessively, or live for their next paycheck. These all-too-common traits make up a scarcity mentality. Money, like everything else in life, is a vibrational energy that needs to flow to grow. Just like water that sits in the same place for too long, if money is stuck in one place with no locomotion, it doesn't flow; it rots.

Recognizing and shifting your mentality has the power to dramatically change your reality. Everything you experience as your outer reality is a direct reflection of your inner beliefs. As philosopher Ernest Holmes explains, "The material world reflects the forms of thought which the Soul holds before it. Life not only responds to your belief, it responds after the manner of your believing, as you believe. It is like a mirror reflecting the image of your belief."[2] Put simply, if you feel dissatisfied with your life, transforming it begins with changing your mind.

> *Your reality is a direct reflection of your inner beliefs, and you can change whatever you believe.*

Whatever you see and experience is merely a product of what's inside of you. So, if you're projecting that you are a magnet to money, you feel great about money, and money loves you, then of course you'll experience financial abundance pouring into your outer reality. Positive thoughts, aligned with feelings and actions, materialize the abundance you desire.

Actions, which we'll get to later in the book, are the daily rituals that, with consistency, propel you toward manifesting your goals: working smart, not hard, in your career choices, stepping outside of your comfort zone every single day, waking up early to begin your day powerfully before everyone else, spending your time productively, and swapping partying and drinking for consistently striving toward your dreams are all aligned steps that will help you achieve your goals faster. Working three hours a day on a new business idea equates to 1,095 hours per year of precious attention devoted to your dreams. How incredible is that? And then, just like magic, you're at the top of your game and your side hustle becomes your main hustle, generating more income than you thought possible.

Of course, focusing on improving your skills is fundamental to becoming the best at what you do. Focus your attention (which will filter into your subconscious mind) on your ability to do the thing that you are best at and that you are therefore monetizing. The greatest minds on the planet, from Albert Einstein to Leonardo Di Vinci and Pablo Picasso, would spend time away from the world, in their own secluded space, honing in on their craft and focusing on forever improving their skill set, becoming the best in the world at what they did. That's no different than you and me. Find a place and time every day to become a master of your artistry. What is your unique skill set? What is the craft you want to focus on? Get really clear on this answer. If you are not constantly learning, you are dying, and if you are not earning, you are depreciating. If you are not creating, you are disintegrating, and if you are not believing, you are shrinking—shrinking to fit those past limiting beliefs and those petty labels you've attached to yourself or allowed others to stick to you like little yellow sticky notes. You are so much more than that, and it is time to peel those sticky notes off and rise up to be the version of you that you deserve to be.

Throughout the past decade, there have been numerous scientific and psychological studies that have revealed the importance of our early years. According to The National Academies of Science, Engineering, and Medicine, "Early childhood is a time when developmental changes are happening that can have profound and lasting consequences for a child's future."[3] Everything that a child experiences or is exposed to at a young age, specifically until age seven, has a profound impact on their development, mindset, and future. "Even in their earliest years, children are starting to learn about their world in sophisticated ways that are not always reflected in their outward behavior. Learning and development for young children is both rapid and cumulative, continuously laying a foundation for later learning."[4] Studies show that everything we absorb during those early years, positive or negative, including how money is regarded, gets imprinted into our subconscious minds. Later, those beliefs start to become us, cementing into the very foundations of our identity.

Your beliefs are ingrained without you even realizing it. The good news is that they are not irreplaceable. You can rewire your subconscious mind and write a new outcome. You can transform those discouraging energies about money into a new outcome of wealth and abundance. You can become the author of your own story. The very first thing to do, and you can do this right now, is write down your money story. What are your feelings about money? What statements about money have been hardwired into your mind when you dive a little deeper? Whatever you write down is a map of your relationship with money. This map will help you outline your limiting beliefs and shine a light on where to place your focus to shift your mindset toward wealth and abundance. Whatever you write down will also help you through the practices that follow. Take some time now to jot everything down and keep this list handy.

If you find yourself expressing something along the lines of always losing money, thinking money doesn't like you, you can never make enough of it, or you never had enough growing up, this is the perfect time to transmute those beliefs into a new, abundant mindset and install your new wealth consciousness. And right here, right now, I'm going to tell you how. Using my world-renowned, scientifically proven MBS method, we'll approach both the subconscious and conscious mind to generate new, long-term positive changes to your mindset—and thus, to your life. All the tools necessary to make such an enormous impact in your life are right here in this book.

Understanding and learning to navigate your own mind can facilitate astoundingly rapid achievement of your most desired goals and dreams. If you've ever been to one of my talks or have read my previous book, you know how much I love to geek out on the brain. The Reticular Activating System (RAS), for example, is a network of neurons located in the lower part of your brain. It's the Editor and Chief of evaluation and filtration of all incoming information and prioritizing what we deem important. And what gets flagged as important? Anything you focus your mind on!

The RAS filters over two million bits of data through our senses every second like a great viaduct, bridging the gap between our subconscious and conscious mind. Our RAS allows us to filter out any irrelevant noise when we're in a crowded place so we're able to focus on a single conversation. When your name is being called at an airport, for example, your RAS is responsible for your ability to recognize it, despite being oblivious to any prior calls over the speaker. This filtering of information prevents us from being overstimulated by the avalanche of data we receive every second of every day. But here's the best part, what you focus on expands. So, if you consciously *choose* to give attention to something specific, your RAS will filter out anything unrelated to serving that purpose. You can think of it akin to upgrading your mind to the premium subscription of a music or streaming service, removing any annoying ads that risk robbing your attention from manifesting greatness. As Dr. William Horton says, "You can deliberately reprogram the Reticular Activating System by self choosing the exact messages you send from your conscious mind."[5] By getting consciously specific with your RAS, you'll be able to target both your subconscious and conscious mind, instigating all the changes you wish to see in your life.

So, back to the main question, what does your brain flag as important? Anything you focus your mind on is what your

RAS prioritizes as important to you. Let's take the example of focusing your attention on the belief that you are not worthy of money, or that money doesn't like you. Of course, your RAS is going to surround you with evidence to prove that belief system to be true. You experience endless occurrences, circumstances, people, and places that prove your lack and the scarcity of money.

If you're able to gain an awareness of this without judgment, you unlock the power to replace your limiting beliefs and rewrite the outcome through the mere recognition of what it is you'd like to shift. By embodying your newfound positive, abundant, affirmative beliefs around money (money loves me, I am worthy of abundance, I am worthy of financial freedom, I love making money, I am successful), your RAS will continue to respond accordingly, providing you with a sea of evidence to prove that belief system is real. Constantly recurring opportunities, events, people, and places that back up your new belief system will pop up all around you.

It's a bit ironic because similar to your RAS filter canceling out all that extra noise, those opportunities that are suddenly so apparent were always there. You just didn't know where to look—or perhaps you weren't ready to. Now you are. Now you're ready to see these enriching and empowering opportunities in all their glory with the knowledge that they originate within your own subconscious mind. By reprogramming your subconscious and continuously installing your new wealth mindset, you affirm you are worthy of abundance, riches, and making an impactful contribution to the world. All will come to fruition because those beliefs will be ingrained into your being on a subconscious level, so much so that your conscious mind will begin to carve pathways to materialize these beliefs into your reality.

Focus on abundance, focus on wealth, focus on health, focus on joy, focus on your limitless powers and capabilities to do great things in this world. The only limitations you really have are the boundaries you've built in your own mind. The only limitations to abundant wealth are the scarcity beliefs you've managed to implement in one way or another. Every single one of you was put on this planet to experience all the beauty life has to offer.

You are meant to be wealthy. It's your birthright to be healthy, abundant, vibrant, harmonious, and confident. You are meant to have all these things and more, because the more wealth you create, the more resources you'll have to share, help others, and positively impact the world. Perhaps you decide to build an orphanage, an animal foundation, an entity to help people with diseases, or supply those with no basic resources. You might create your own charity. And if it weren't for money, you wouldn't have the means to help in such great proportions. You are meant for riches too. Don't allow yourself to get swept into the hamster cycle like generations before you. Jump right off that hamster wheel and say, "Now is my time to change the trajectory for the future generations."

Being wealthy will transform your life, your children's lives, your grandchildren's lives, and thousands, perhaps even millions of people's lives long after you've departed this earth. You see, you want to make sure that anything you desire, you're seeking for the betterment of others. Create to serve and help others, add value to people's lives, help them improve, motivate and empower them, or enhance their quality of their life in some way. Wanting things that serve the greater collective and better the lives of those around you, even after you're gone, is the essence of leaving a legacy. That's the real manifestation.

Having a prosperous financial outlook is key to creating a life of wealth. There are six core principles of building wealth that I'm going to share with you so that you too can be confident and assertive when climbing the ladder to financial freedom.

The first fundamental principle is one we've already been through: having your mindset on point. As I've explained throughout this chapter, the correct mindset will attract abundance, wealth, and possibilities to you. Remember, eradicating your limiting beliefs and scarcity mindset is the first step toward creating wealth.

The second principle is having a holistic view of your finances. This will help you understand all the pieces that make up your unique financial puzzle. Everything is interconnected, and it all pieces together to form a panoramic view of your financial life. Every decision has an impact, so when you think about your finances broadly and understand your short-term, mid-term, and long-term financial goals, you'll be able to make decisions in a much more efficient and precise manner.

The third principle is measuring the effectiveness of your assets, investments, and expenses. Evaluating your financial decisions will also help you make smarter decisions overall. What are your liabilities, assets, and cash flow? What is the real cost of using one strategy over another? What's the actual return of each investment you're currently making?

The fourth principle is to turn your focus onto your cash flow. As I mentioned, money, like all energies, must flow to grow. This means that locking up your money in an account or a qualified plan or anywhere where you can't easily access or use it will massively limit your ability to enlarge your wealth. When it comes to cash flow, it is very important that it's constantly moving in and through in different ways, such as investments that will come back to you in greater proportions. Circulating your money will considerably fast-track your wealth-building, because it will eventually create different sources of income that allow for a prosperous, abundant life fueled by financial freedom.

Principle number five is taking control of your money. Where does your money come from? Where does your money go? What are your financial habits? Knowing this will help you regain power over your finances and make better decisions. The quantity of your cash flow doesn't matter. As long as you have it under your control, you have nothing to lose. Avoid losing your money to high-risk businesses, taxation, management fees, or qualified plans.

The sixth and final principle is leverage. Leveraging allows you to make more with less and increase the productivity of a single dollar; therefore, you will be able to dramatically maximize your return on investment—and your overall wealth in the long run.

> *Success is a mindset, not the amount in your bank account. Money is just a by-product of success, so don't go after the money. Go after the success and how it can change lives and solve problems for people. Then the money will flow to you abundantly.*

Ultimately, when it comes to building wealth, it all sums up to this: the more problems you solve, the more money you make. You want to create something you truly believe in, something that serves a greater purpose. Once you know what you want to create, you'll have to reverse engineer (starting from where you want to be) the amount of money that you want to make. Find people who have already achieved what you want. What did they do? How did they get there? Create a clear vision of that outcome. As Napoleon Hill says, "Whatever the mind can conceive and believe, it can achieve."

The Law of Compensation states that you receive what you give. We'll be diving deeper into understanding this law in the coming chapters. Ralph Waldo Emerson explained, "Each person is compensated in like manner for that which he or she has contributed." In other words, you reap what you sow. No matter how small or big your acts of service, they will always be rewarded in the same quantity. Money works the same way. The amount of money that you earn through your own creation is exactly proportionate to:

a) The identified problem or need
b) The value you are creating and delivering
c) The uniqueness of your product or service
d) The amount of the identified problem or need you are solving

Figuring out this ratio will allow you to create something of so much value that the impact you'll create and the lives you'll be able to change will be both exceptional and indispensable. This certifies that the more problems you solve for others, the more money you'll make.

Becoming a multimillionaire or a billionaire doesn't just happen. You don't just suddenly wake up to find a million dollars in your bank account. Getting your mindset right first and creating new, positive habits like the multimillionaires you look up to is what will take you where you want to be. Your mindset makes up 80 percent of your success; your aligned actions make up the other 20 percent. Newton's third law states that for every action there is always an equal reaction. Success is a reaction to the actions you choose to take, or as I like to say, success is a reaction to your actions.

Chapter 2:

Letting Go to Grow

L etting go can be a very difficult thing to do. As humans, we're inherently taught to hold onto the things that we're assured belong to us, to the things we love or have loved, to cling to our most precious memories from fear that if we loosen our grip, we risk losing them forever. What most people fail to recognize is that what we hoard over time may constitute that weight on our shoulders—that baggage that's keeping you from growing and blossoming into your best self. Letting go is the act of surrendering to the present moment just as it is, allowing that inner pressure pot, that horrible weight on your chest, to cease. It's finally taking a gloriously deep breath again with a sense of relief, peace, and freedom, allowing you to flow through your life lightly, making growth a process of effortless ease.

Quantum mechanics shows us that everything carries an energy, and every thought has a vibrational frequency. When you accumulate physical things, for example, you absorb the energies emitted by those objects, regardless of whether they serve you or not. In fact, they might have stopped serving you a long time ago, but you can't part with them because they are reminiscent of someone or something in particular. But memories do not lie within objects. People we've lost are not found within the things they had. Our experiences are not stored in the souvenirs we returned with. The true essence of all of it is within us, and once you understand that, you'll gain the ability to let go of external things and move forward.

Many people can't get their heads around why manifestation isn't happening for them, why life just isn't "going their way," or why achieving their goals seems like such a struggle. Take a moment to explore this idea. Write your thoughts down.

After you've illuminated these mindset blockages, you'll be ready to take your first step toward your future. Gaining conscious awareness of your current situation gives you control over your life. It opens the door to release blockages, to forgive others, and most importantly, to forgive yourself. You'll be ready to embark on the journey of letting go.

When you go through something as traumatic as a sexual abuse, like I did, your brain and body respond in unprecedented ways. Your emotional and psychological self can become completely shattered to the point where you feel like an outsider in your own life. A sense of confusion, victimization, and self-loathing can overcome you. You might find yourself digging an endless hole of self-sabotage, self-blame, despair, hatred, and rage to the point that you might even get sick. Processing trauma requires all the strength inside your being. Our brains are designed to do anything to make us feel comfortable or at peace, so it decides to ignore, forget, and bury trauma that is difficult to process and heal.

Accepting that a traumatic situation happened is often the hardest part. And understanding that what happened was in no way your fault can seem like an impossible task. When something severe happens to you, you feel so ashamed and hurt that it's difficult to share what happened even with your own family and closest friends. So, you find yourself holding on to rage and resentment that builds up inside of you and asphyxiates you and you end up doing some stupid things to cope.

For me, it was drugs. I had gotten myself into a mental state of self-hatred that I could no longer bear. I was ashamed of what happened, of people seeing me and judging me, of my body, of being myself in any way. I was holding onto this secret that filled me with pain, and the only way I felt relief was through drugs. I thought drugs were the way out, when, in reality, they just pulled me down even further. I kept lying to my family and my friends, telling them I was okay and nothing was going on, but I was slowly being consumed by drugs and was constantly seeking ways to economically sustain this addiction without people noticing. The result? I became a webcam girl.

I didn't think about the huge consequences this would imply for my family, friends, and myself. Instead, I thought that it was the perfect way to sustain my addiction. Entering that male-driven industry rapidly snowballed into exploiting my body in so many ways for others' sake. To say I was unhappy is an understatement. My coping had gotten way out of control, and my anxiety and depression were slowly killing me. It was not sustainable. It had never been sustainable.

My mind had tricked me into believing I could do everything on my own. I thought I was in control of my decisions and, therefore, of my life. The truth is that I needed help—urgently. I needed a light to guide the way, a light greater than myself.

Some years later, after I had my son, I was hit with an illness because I had exploited my body for so long. I thought my trauma could be left in the past, but it was so deeply rooted within me that I had allowed it to define me. My unhealed self had finally caught up with me, and it wouldn't go unnoticed. That is until I discovered and created my MBS Method. This method was the only way I could finally heal from the traumas that had haunted me for years. Why? Because I finally learned to *let go* and forgive. I released all the pain, all the anger, and all the guilt I had hoarded inside of me throughout the years, and I was finally able to open that space for better things.

Forgiving and detaching from old, dried-up energies is the first step to attracting great things into your life. Doing this repeatedly has been the source of my strength for letting go of the deeply scarring traumas I went through as a young teenage girl. Though now an empowered confident women, having lived in my dream houses around the world, met my soulmate, and existing in a happy and harmonious relationship, I began my journey as a scared, frail young woman overpowered by experiences of sexual abuse.

If it wasn't for forgiveness, none of my transformation would have been possible. If I had continued holding onto those traumatic experiences, I would have become a product of my past. My trauma would still define my identity. And there's no freaking way I'm going to let my adversities stand in the way of my present or my future.

Yes, those experiences, as awful as they were, are part of my story and taught me important lessons that contribute to the person I am today. **But they do not dictate the direction of my future.** Bearing burdens and living anything other than my greatest life is not my destiny. And neither is yours.

If you're reading this now and feel you're carrying a burden or trauma around with you, baggage so heavy you might find it difficult to walk, know that you're not alone. Millions of people around the world, myself included, have endured immense suffering—and have found the strength to let go of it. Today's your day. Now is your chance to let go of that pain, set down that burden. Release it from your body, release it from your entire being, and leave it right there on the road behind you.

We are vessels of energy and information, filled with the experiences, beliefs, and relationships built throughout our lives. We carry all our old traumas, our limiting beliefs that keep us from becoming our best selves and attracting the life we desire, floating on the surface of our consciousness. To expand your vessel and receive more from the Universe, you must make space for new things to come into your life by focusing on removing the blockages that are getting in the way of living as your highest self and fulfilling your destiny.

Through my MBS method, masses of people have had the opportunity to release burdens, trauma, and painful memories. As you now know, releasing from the conscious mind isn't enough; you need to let go on a subcellular level. Your subconscious mind is the head architect, sculpting your reality into what appears to your conscious mind as a total coincidence. Do you understand how light you'll feel once you let go of that burden? Do you understand the freedom you'll experience once you leave that burden behind and stop letting it control you? It feels so good to let go.

As amazing as it feels to release pain and trauma, you must understand that the only person feeling those things in the first place is you. No one else feels your trauma like you do. So, it's up to you to let go of it. When you don't forgive, that person or situation you are holding onto seizes control of your life and continues strolling through it, day after day. The other person might not even know, or care, that you feel this way. They just move on.

Now I'm not saying you have to forget what happened; I am inviting you to *forgive* it. Once you release the old, negative energy from your body, you'll feel like a renewed being.

You will literally feel pounds lighter! Some people may even say you're glowing or ask if you changed your hair. In truth, nothing physically about you will have changed, but a powerful change *will* occur within you. Interior changes invigorate every cell in your body; transformation ripples through you on a cellular level, causing a shift in the very nature of your DNA.

Releasing negative energy is the equivalent of performing a sort of biohacking self-surgery, extracting any cells that don't align with your higher purpose. When you undergo surgery to remove a cancerous tumor or your appendix, for instance, you're freeing your body of disease, removing potentially fatal disruptions from your system. When your body falls out of homeostasis—a state of balance, positivity, and health—it enters a state of dis-ease, and that's when many health problems begin to spiral. There's always a root cause for our health problems, often beyond our comprehension. Nevertheless, you should always attempt to pinpoint the primary cause of any sort of physical pain. What is your body trying to tell you? What does it represent? Chakras can be a helpful guide to better understand central energy channels in your body. For example, when your throat is sore, it may be a great opportunity for you to evaluate how you're showing up and speaking your truth, if at all. Maybe you've felt underappreciated, unheard, or ignored in the past. Or perhaps you've swallowed thoughts or feelings that were better off being expressed. Physical health problems always come down to something deeper.

To truly grow, you have to learn to fully let go and clear space for the arrival of the new. The universal law of growth suggests that unlike our height, reaching its maximum around age eighteen, we're continuously growing as far as our personal development is concerned. This law is made up of three fundamental aspects according to John C. Maxwell: intention, awareness, and consistency.[6] By growing, we keep ourselves alive. If we are not actively growing and seeking to learn new things, both spiritually and psychologically, we're dying.

The question is: are you ready to let go? Are you ready to start forgiving and releasing? Are you truly ready? Because every day you have the choice to either let go or hold on, stay alive or stand in line waiting for death to come knocking at your door.

Chapter 3:

The Magic of Forgiveness

T o release your past traumas and step into your full potential, you must first learn to forgive yourself and others. As I mention in the previous chapter, many of us have allowed anger and resentment to build up for so long that we might even be oblivious to carrying it. Resentment rots us from the inside out, dominating our reality with negative energies that will never serve us. Dr. Nina Radcliff explains how resentment can weigh you down, causing serious health implications in the long run: "Resentment can weaken your immune system while increasing stress and anxiety and the risk of heart disease, hypertension, stroke, cancer, alcoholism, drug addiction, compulsive behavior, weight gain, mood swings, depression and burnout, and it's been linked to a shortened lifespan. In close relationships, resentment destroys trust and intimacy, fuels power struggles or persistent passive aggression and eventually leads to contempt and detachment."[7]

In my case, my previous relationships revealed so much unhealed pain and resentment. I remember that I would endlessly battle with my partners about the same things over and over again. It was as if I was copying and pasting the same relationships for years, bouncing between pushing my partners away and running from them in an exhausting loop on the road to nowhere. The penny dropped when I finally understood that the common denominator was me. The issue didn't span from my partners; it was clear this battle was one between me, myself, and I.

All the frustration, disappointment, pain, neglect, harm, abuse, and mistreatment I'd experienced and hadn't forgiven myself for resulted in a slow-rolling snowball that morphed into a negative emotional avalanche called resentment. I held that resentment inside of me, and the worst part was, I was projecting it onto the people closest to me. Untreated pain and downright rage toward myself and my father infected my romantic relationships. I'd attract partners who mirrored memories of my father, replaying his mistreatment of my mother in my reality. The only outlet I had for my pain landed me in horrible confrontations with my romantic partners. Looking back, it was my defense mechanism, an unconscious blurting out of everything I never got to say to my father. What's worse, I continuously added weight to my resentment for each partner for every behavior that was, in truth, a reflection of my father's.

I yo-yoed from fiancé to singleton, to being married, to being divorced. It took me years to be able to write this down on paper and open up about it, with the hope that my story may keep you from making the same self-sabotaging mistakes over and over again. It's okay to release that pain you've been holding onto. It's okay to forgive yourself for everything you wish you'd done differently. It's okay to recognize that sometimes you've mistreated yourself and others. It is okay to admit you've been harmed, mistreated, neglected, or belittled. Surrendering to all those adversities will only make you stronger.

Some people's breakdowns end up being the very source of their breakthroughs, often sparked from a traumatic experience, just like I was during the most horrendous year of my life. Others might experience a life-changing epiphany during a moment of joy, euphoria, or what can only be described as pure bliss. Simply being here, reading this, proves you are ready to forgive yourself and others and move forward to manifest all you want in your life. This book in your hands is the sign that you're on the cusp of a breakthrough. Perhaps you're already living abundantly in one area of your life but lacking in another, feeling a niggle that something's still missing. Practice forgiveness, either for someone else or yourself.

Like the cycle of self-sabotage I had unconsciously fallen into with my relationships, destructive behavior has the potential to pop up in any area of your life. Learn to recognize when something's out of alignment—a codependent relationship, a self-sabotaging habit, vicious cycles—and evaluate what or who it is you need to forgive. Cast your mind back to your childhood, unpacking anything that could have planted that seed of resentment. Whenever you get that negative feeling, pause, accept it, analyze it, and remind yourself that it doesn't have to be that way.

Lao Tzu said, "When the student is ready, the teacher will appear." Picking up this book was no coincidence; it's a clear sign you're ready to be guided through your pain and live the abundant life you desire. The exercises and methods I share in this book helped me during my own healing journey. They taught me to let go, forgive, and live a life free of pain, traumas, and resentment. Since I didn't have someone to guide me through those profoundly traumatic experiences, I wrote my own guidebook and propelled myself toward this quantum field of abundance, bliss, and harmony. Now, I want to share that with you.

Through deep meditation, self-hypnosis, and specific ancient breathing exercises (i.e., my MBS method), I was able to rewire my neural pathways to become empowered enough to own my identity, clearly define myself, and let go of my past. The first exercise I want to share with you is a mindful meditation, where you will be able to access your deepest emotions, thoughts, and beliefs. I will lay out each step for you, then you can close your eyes and continue on your own.

Read the following paragraphs, and then find the time and space to immerse yourself in what I'm sharing with you.

Get comfortable in this present moment. Take a seat or lie down on your back. Take a deep breath and focus only on your breathing for the next three minutes. Inhale for four seconds, hold for six seconds, and exhale for eight seconds. Each breath should be deeper than the one before and should bring more oxygen to your lungs and your entire body. Feel your diaphragm expanding and contracting, controlling your exhale with each and every breath. Breathe deeply; elongate your exhalation.

As you start to practice this, your mind will start to quiet, your thoughts will dissolve, and your heart will soften. Allow relaxation to fully take over your body. Open the gate into your higher mind faculties to access pure knowledge and download any messages from your higher intelligence. We want to eradicate all the things holding you back from your destiny, all the things stopping you from stepping into fullness and greatness with power and ease.

With each inhale, feel love, gratitude, and excitement entering your being, and with each exhale, focus on letting go of anything no longer serving you. You are safe. It's all okay. It's just me and you now. Exhale, bringing to your mind all the pain, the resentment, the anger, the past. Imagine it physically leaving your body, perhaps in the form of thick black smoke. Keep repeating this. Inhale compassion; exhale pain. Inhale forgiveness and let go a little more with each exhale. With every breath, you allow yourself to dive a little deeper into your subconscious mind. If a thought arises, simply acknowledge it, smile, and let it go.

Now, invite into your mind someone or something that has hurt you. What do you feel? Continue breathing and decide to forgive that person or that situation. Say, "I forgive you. I forgive you. I forgive you." Keep breathing and tell them, "You no longer control me. The only one who has power over my life is me." As you inhale, place one hand over your heart and one hand on your abdomen. Feel your body rise and fall. Now repeat, "I am grateful for you, and I send you love. I forgive you." Breathe in love, compassion, and grace. Now, as you exhale, smile. Fully surrender to this moment and let go. Inhale the feeling of love. Let that spread around your entire body. Understand that even the most direct harm is not personal toward you. Remember that everything a person says and does is a direct reflection of who they are—not of who you are. Forgive them now and repeat, "I am grateful for you, and I send you love. I forgive you now."

Imagine you are glowing with a bright light around you and extend those feelings as far as you can with your next exhale, illuminating the space you're in right now, across your home, across the town, across the state, across the nation, across the world! When you glow, you light up the world around you.

As you learn to forgive everyone and yourself, you evolve into a forgiving person, a compassionate person, a person filled with love and light. It won't just be an exercise you do; it will be who you are, the sheer makeup of your biology. By deciding to forgive today, you're harnessing the frequency of love and gratitude that is your birthright. Today you are making a decision to forgive your past, forgive your parents, forgive the people who hurt you, and forgive yourself.

Now, come back to your breath and slowly open your eyes, with a gentle smile beaming all the way from your lower abdomen up through the top of your head.

Doing this exercise daily will help you release any negative energies holding you back. Through repetition, constantly reprogramming your mindset, you can change your beliefs about your past, learn to let go, and alter your destiny. It's almost as good as going back in time and altering the event itself. If you commit to doing this every day for the next thirty days, you will feel a huge shift in your life and visibly see a change in your outer reality. After just one session, you learn how to release years of pent-up, resentful feelings and forgive. You might already be starting to feel the effectiveness of the exercise. How great does it feel to forgive?

I wrote this section of the book really close to my birthday. Something I love doing when people ask me what I want for my birthday is telling them to write on a little piece of paper what they would like to bless me with, whether it be health, wealth, love, abundance, etc. I want to do this with you now. Write down on a piece of paper what it is you'd like to be blessed with in your life and carry it with you all day. Whenever you open it and read it, receive it as if you were given a gift, like your dream car, a pair of shoes, or a perfume from a dear friend. Feel and receive it as if what's written down is already yours! I also want to invite you to do this for others and light up their hearts. The Universe will pay you back for your kindness and selflessness. You can also gift yourself and those you love with some of my guided meditations and more practical exercises by claiming your free gift at: www.natashagraziano.com/freegift.

When I experienced the most traumatic year of my life to date and realized I was in dire need of help, I started doing this practice every single day until I healed. In my first year of healing, I not only healed myself of my illness but I also made my first million dollars—in under one year of using these practices. I still use the MBS method every day; it's a habit now, and habits form who we are. In fact, science says that by the age of thirty-five, we are just a collation of all the habits we've formulated over the years, so choose wisely. Now you know how. Reading this book is step one. Anyone can change their life for the better and live abundantly simply by following the teachings and methods this book has to offer.

We are all a work in progress, constantly needing to forgive ourselves and others, continuously learning to be more compassionate to achieve our goals faster and easier. The moment you wake up tomorrow, I want you to try something new. Start by saying how grateful you are for each and every thing you have and are. Rejoice in how much you love everything in your life. Be grateful for your breath, your body, and your soul. Be grateful that you are a forgiving person. Give thanks for all the people who surround and uplift you every single day and for those who have taught you lessons that have helped you grow. Express gratitude for the comfort of your bed. Be grateful to have a home, for everything you own. Feel love rise within you and pour out of you as you do this.

When you wake up, place your hands on your heart
and repeat the following words out loud:
I love my life.
I love my home.
I am safe.
I am happy.

This gratitude exercise is actually a great method for calming anxiety as well. You can repeat it anytime, anywhere, as often as you need to. I go deeper into this in another chapter, but for now, just focus on that mantra and continue repeating it every day during your mindful meditation or simply whenever you need to calm your body and mind, allowing yourself to forgive, let go, and open new channels for expansion.

Now that you've learned the tools to let go of the blockages you've been carrying around all these years, it's up to you to start applying them into every area of your life. I'm so proud of you. You've created the space to attract everything you need to become the new, vibrant you and achieve your goals faster.

Chapter 4:

The Secret of the MBS Method

So, what is the MBS method? The Meditational Behavioral Synchronicity method is something I discovered and created; it was what helped me transform my life and the lives of many others, yours included if you are open to receiving it. Through a combination of ancient practices, scientifically driven modalities backed up by numerous studies, and alignment techniques, I unlocked the key to abundance in every area of my life. Each tool became a key ingredient of my MBS method, a method that can effortlessly spark everlasting change into your life as it did mine, opening the gate for overflowing plenitude in every aspect.

In the book *The Power of Your Subconscious Mind*, Joseph Murphy writes: "The way to get rid of darkness is with light. The way to overcome cold is with heat. The way to overcome the negative thought is to substitute the good thought, affirm the good, and the bad will vanish."[8] This part of the book struck a chord in me when I first read it. Enraptured by every word, I realized, for the first time in my life, that the way to attract and create anything and everything I wanted was simple. I had to eliminate my negative thoughts or beliefs and replace them with positive ones. I immediately started researching how I could achieve that for myself. A lot of people assume that just saying "oh, I'll get rid of it" will cause negativity to magically vanish, but that's not how it works at all. To eliminate potentially years of pent-up negativity, a certain level of commitment must be made to "doing the work" inside and out. We're not born negative; negativity is learned through direct experience, so, in order to change and eventually eliminate negativity, we must get to the root of the problem.

Having lost everything to my name in the space of a year, it was crystal clear that the only place left to look to find the answers to all my prayers was within me. When my outer reality crumbled, I knew I'd never regain sight of the path unless I committed to healing internally—for both my son and myself—to find my way out of the darkest hole I'd ever visited. I embarked on my mission to not only tap into *my* unlimited human potential but also to do it in a way that allowed me to pass on the wisdom and help others tap into their power. I researched neuroscience, learned from yogis, and explored various methods and practices. My research taught me a lifetime's worth of lessons about discovering who I really am, and I felt both awakened and enlightened by the MBS method.

In the first year of my comeback, I gained the tools, the confidence, and the power to start becoming my highest self. I was no longer broke. I spoke to tens of thousands of people every year on stages around the globe. I pinched myself sometimes, thinking, "Can it really be me achieving all these great things?"

And it was. It was me *becoming* my best self.

Fast-forward to today, and I am a Wall Street Journal Best Selling Author of this book *Be It Until You Become It* and also my presence on social media has increased dramatically. You see, the thing is, if people like you, they become receptive to the wisdom you're providing. They let you take their hand and guide them toward their best selves. Being "likable" has allowed me to get where I am today. Serving people across the world as my dharma, my life's purpose, is the greatest gift. Being chosen to spread positivity, love, life hacks, and the MBS Method is the biggest blessing I could have wished for.

When I'm helping people transform their mindset through my one-on-one coaching or my online programs, I remind them that my teachings can only provide them with the essential toolkit they need to take action. The real solution, the magic, is already within them. My teachings have proven time and time again that once those initial limiting beliefs have lifted, the MBS method empowers you to heal and transform any area of your life. Once we have the tools, once we make space to build that bridge, we can start walking toward anything we desire, constantly growing our confidence to run across that bridge into the abundance of joy, light, and love that's waiting for us.

> *Meditational: Ancient breathing; Holotropic practices that create altered states of awareness and align you to greater receptivity of transformation.*

All living things breathe. Breathing is the basis of our existence on this planet; yet, most of us breathe incorrectly. Somewhere along the way we learned to breathe from our chest. Our breathing became shallow, potentially due to the increased anxiety and stress that comes with the daily demands of adult life. For the majority of us, both children and adults alike, "natural breathing" appears as a lifting of the shoulders with each inhale and a collapsing of them with each exhale. Correct, functional breathing originates from the diaphragm and involves an activation of the lower ribs, allowing the lungs to expand and contract to their optimal capacity, which, according to the American Lung Association, is about six liters of air (like three large soda bottles) during both rest and physical exercise. Correct breathing promotes a release of tension from the secondary breathing muscles, your neck and shoulders, for example. As ironic as it may sound, breathing isn't supposed to be difficult. If you look at the way a baby breathes, you'll notice their little belly gently expanding and contracting in an effortless wave with every gentle breath in and out of their tiny body. Babies have much to teach us in the art of breathing, and it may take some conscious practice to relearn how to breathe properly as an adult. Fortunately, our poor breathing habits are not of genetic origin; we learned them, and it's time to start unlearning.

I stumbled upon ancient diaphragmatic breathing in a peculiar turn of events during my late teenage years in Cyprus. Most of my family was born and raised in the mountains of Cyprus, and most of them still live there to this day. As a teenager, I'd take a trip every summer to visit my family, and as a somewhat rebellious teenager, this wasn't always the ideal plan in my eyes. To be honest, I remember dreading the thought of going there again, facing what felt like such an alien culture. So, you could imagine my initial response when my parents announced they were sending me to a monastery to fully immerse myself in my inherited culture at the age of eighteen.

At eighteen, a whole summer spent on what I assumed would be doing nothing in a monastery felt like a complete nightmare. But as the days passed, I began to understand why I'd been sent there. I remember one day especially clearly. We were out taking one of our regular walks up the mountain, the sun gleaming but the air cold, and something jolted my attention. I heard my name being called so loudly I couldn't help but separate myself from the group and walk toward the voice. I saw a lone man, sitting on the grass, his eyes closed, his legs crossed, and his arms peacefully laying on his knees. He seemed to be at such ease. It was one of the most peaceful scenes I had ever witnessed.

I dared to walk closer and closer, astonished by what I was seeing. I had never seen anything like it. It was as if my sight had veered into portrait mode, everything around me seemingly fading, my gaze fixated on the man sitting alone on the grass.

"Do you mind if I sit next to you?" I said, finally allowing my words to break the silence, "You have such a peaceful and powerful energy."

He opened his eyes, and with a smile, patted the floor beside him, indicating that it was okay for me to accompany him in whatever exactly he was doing.

He closed his eyes again and continued with what appeared to be incredibly intense breathing. His face was beaming. He looked like he had reached another dimension. I watched in awe, desperate to know what this was all about. I wanted to embody that powerful energy he was radiating so beautifully. I suddenly understood I was there for a reason and intended to learn as much as I could from this mysterious man.

When his practice appeared to be over, he slowly opened his eyes and turned his head to look at me. "I am 105 years old," he said. He didn't look that age at all. I opened my eyes in surprise. "I've had no disease, no reduced senses, no fatigue . . . I've just learned how to breathe," he claimed, softly, a lifetime of wisdom behind his words. I was so intrigued. I thought breathing was something that didn't need to be learned! In my mind, everyone did it naturally. What could there be to learn about?

As we got to talking, the yogi explained that our breath determines our life span. "Breath can heal you and feed you," he said. He spoke of the importance of taking deep, controlled breaths and how breathing impacts every area of our lives. He described his own personal experience and how breathing exercises had helped him survive and overcome various circumstances throughout his life, proclaiming that he owed his long, healthy life to the sheer act of breathing. I was fascinated.

"I want to learn how to do this," I said after hours of endless talking. I almost begged him to teach me his breathing exercises. And so, he did. I felt free. I felt empowered, as if I could do everything and anything I wanted. My anxiety ceased, my nerves faded, everything in my life appeared so much clearer.

I woke up the next day and the only thing playing on repeat in my mind were those enriching moments with the wise yogi the day before. I rushed up the mountain hoping to find him again, and there he was. I went through the breathing exercises once more and realized I didn't want to leave the monastery anymore. I'd discovered so much through this enlightened being. I just wanted to learn as much as I could from him. Every day I went back and practiced the ancient pranayama breathing exercises he taught me. Slowly and steadily, I began to get the hang of it. Every time I practiced, I felt like a higher realm of consciousness opened for my free exploration, giving me endless peace and possibilities, and it was all due to correct, deep breathing.

The repeatedly astounding effects the wise teachings of the yogi had on me were later confirmed in studies. Dr. Xiao-Xi

Zhang and Dr. Zu-Hai Zhao explained that "the impact of breathing exercises on oxygen–carbon dioxide homeostasis via normal breathing is crucial for health while disturbance of the homeostasis may cause many disorders, especially cancers."[9] Pranayama ancient breathing techniques also develop a stronger connection between our body and mind over time, keeping us in alignment and balance. These methods, originating from yoga practices in India, have positive effects on the immune system, cognitive function, lung capacity, emotional regulation, anxiety, and stress management while also being effective in reducing psychosomatic disorders like high blood pressure and migraines.

Ancient breathwork shows up throughout history across a vast sea of cultures: Chinese medicine, Japanese, Indian, Greek, and Hawaiian philosophies, as well as Tibetan, Amharic, Mayan, Egyptian, and Quechua cultures. Today, these important practices continue to help people live in a heightened state of consciousness. By continuously, ritualistically practicing the breathing exercises I learned in Cyprus, I realized I could face each day with a feeling of gratitude, strength, and optimism. I was ready for anything the world could throw at me. It was a really beautiful thing.

So many years later, when I found myself struggling during the lowest point in my life, feeling completely lost, broken, and hopeless, I remembered that day I met the yogi in Cyprus. My illness was literally killing me, and the thought of not being able to be a mother for my son tormented my waking hours. I was slowly giving up on myself and my life. I remember feeling like healing, like overcoming *that* situation, was impossible, assuming my only way out was simply accepting who I'd become. But something told me I had to reach out to the yogi in Cyprus. So, I gathered my last ounce of strength and wrote him a letter. I didn't have a phone number, but I did have an address I hoped would reach him. I had written to him before, thanking him for all he'd taught me, but never received a reply. Nevertheless, I was desperate, so I decided to write to him. The letter said something along the lines of, "I am going through something in my life right now. I am struggling like never before physically, mentally, spiritually, and emotionally. I feel like I need to talk to you, and I need you to guide me through this. I remember how you taught me about breathing, and you said how deeply breathing heals. So, I'd love to just . . . get in touch with you." I added my cell phone number at the bottom with the hope that by some miracle he would contact me.

A week passed before my phone rang. In great angst, I answered. He hadn't left my mind for a single second since I'd sent the letter. "I will help you. I will show you what to do," he affirmed, almost as soon as I'd said "hello." He reminded me of all the teachings he'd shared with me years ago and guided me through the ancient practice. When I hung up the phone, I continued meditating. I was so thankful for him. After a while, my energy lifted just a fraction; I was feeling better. It was in that precise moment that the "M" of my MBS method was born. I intertwined the ancient knowledge of the yogi with a series of meditations, breathing exercises, Neuro-linguistic programming (NLP), self-hypnosis, and introspective mindfulness practices that I began to do religiously every single day. The synergizing of these modalities created something so deep, so calming, so healing, and so easy to apply that I thought surely this could help other people as it's done for me.

Gradually, my sparkle returned. I felt like myself again—happy and optimistic with clear medical assessments. That girl who was constantly defeated by life had left me. Previously dominating negative thoughts and emotions were merely an afterthought, and miraculously my autoimmune disease ceased to exist. I was stepping into my power at last and becoming who I wanted to be.

Healing, of course, is anything but a linear process. You could liken it to a roller coaster, with soaring highs and crashing lows that hit you in the pit of your stomach, sometimes traveling so fast you lose all sight of any sort of destination. But if you're committed and consistently showing up for yourself, there is no way you won't be healed.

One of my favorite ancient breathing techniques for this healing process is alternate nostril breathing (Nadi Shodhana Pranayama). I repeat this exercise twenty-seven times, because according to ancient gurus and sages, multiples of nine synchronize with our biological rhythms. The way you do it is as follows.

Gently press your thumb on one of your nostrils, inhale through the other one, and then alternate your thumb at the top and exhale with the nostril that was covered initially. So, press your right nostril with your thumb. Exhale and inhale deeply through your left nostril. Hold it while you release your right nostril and press your left nostril with your third finger. Now exhale through your right nostril and inhale again. Hold it while you release your left nostril and go back to the right. Switch back and forth, alternating between your nostrils for any cycle of nine you choose, and feel how your mind begins to clear, and your heart rate slows.

This practice opens the door to tap into your deeper emotions, calms anxiety and stress, and soothes you back into the present moment. I unveiled, and eventually released, so many untreated emotions I had stored deep down within me, keeping me from living my best life, by practicing Nadi Shodhana Pranayama.

There are an infinite number of breathing techniques out there to apply to an array of different intentions—to energize, to concentrate, to sleep deeper, or to connect more authentically with yourself. Some have been utterly transformational for me. You can access each of these meditations through my online portals. I trust that you will actively begin your journey to self-awareness and self-realization through meditation and breathing to uncover your authentic self and who you truly are meant to be. Commit to yourself right now. Commit to the process and acknowledge that you have already committed enough to read this far into this book, so you are ready to heal and take one more step toward the life that's waiting for you.

There is a quote by Joe Dispenza about the power of meditation I adore. He says, "Meditation opens the door between the conscious and subconscious minds. We meditate to enter the operating system of the subconscious, where all of those unwanted habits and behaviors reside, and change them to more productive modes to support us in our lives." Meditation and breathing provide the bridge to tap into your subconscious mind and step toward your new life. I share all of this with you because I want to save you the time and pain of searching for answers and effective ways to make that shift. I wholeheartedly believe in my method because I've seen it work for myself and for so many others; it's what I would've liked to know when I was suffering for all those years.

Behavioral: neuroscience and neuroplasticity

The behavioral aspect of the MBS method refers to the neuroscience behind the Law of Attraction. You might be thinking, "What? The woo-woo spirituality and the science in the same chapter?"

That's right; we're synergizing the two.

As spiritual as I am, I've always had the need to support my beliefs with scientific and medical research that explains how everything works from a biological perspective.

We've already explored the subconscious mind, the conscious mind, and the RAS, which, as you now know, explains how our outer reality is a direct reflection of our unique internal set of beliefs, thoughts, and feelings. We discussed the importance of trading your limiting beliefs for positive ones and creating space for the arrival of the new into your life. You also now recognize the importance of your mindset and being aligned with your thoughts, emotions, and actions to create the life you desire. These are all related to the Law of Attraction—what we are, we attract. We are an accumulation of everything we've allowed into our lives: who we relate with, the conversations we engage in, what we watch, read, and listen to, and what we learn, come to believe, and subsequently do. Because of this, it's vitally important to consciously evaluate what you are feeding your mind. Does it uplift you or support your growth in any way? Or is it something that would be better erased from your life completely?

You see, thoughts don't appear out of thin air. Even one tiny thought has the potential to light up numerous parts of the brain simultaneously. Your brain is like a supercomputer receiving a million pieces of information every second, and the type of information coming through influences the way the brain functions.

Thoughts are often triggered outside of your conscious control. They can be triggered by a specific situation or person, a strong connection, memories, something you watch, hear, or read, something you learn, and the list goes on and on. The magic lies in identifying your personal triggers within your environment. What we can identify, we're able to shift. As you identify your thought triggers, you might feel compelled to change your surroundings, the people you follow on social media, or right down to the types of shows you're watching. You will want to immerse your mind in information that will program it into thinking the way you want it to and get back into the driver's seat of your mind. That way, when you must make a decision and internal neural networks are competing with each other, the network most likely to activate will be a positive one.

According to a recent study performed by scientists at King's College London, "The habit of repetitive negative thinking over a prolonged period of time (RNT) can have a harmful effect on the brain's capacity to think, reason and form memories. RNT is a common behavior in people suffering from depression, anxiety, sleep disorders, post-traumatic stress disorder, and life stress; which are themselves associated with increased risk of Alzheimer's. RNT can occur without us being consciously aware of it and consumes our finite capacity of brain resources. Importantly, RNT also triggers a physical stress response in the brain, which over a prolonged period of time may cause damage and reduce the brain's resilience to Alzheimer's disease."[10] So, negative thinking physically affects our brain's health and performance in the long term with detrimental implications for our quality of life. On the flip side, when we have a positive thought, our ability to concentrate enhances. We're able to better understand information and analyze data more coherently. Positive thoughts also solidify the connection of neurons within the brain, neurons that fire together and wire together, resulting in dramatic uplevelling of cognitive skills like productivity, creativity, and problem-solving.

Our thoughts and emotions influence every single action we take—every choice, every urge—and they ultimately define the course of our lives. Our thoughts signal for neurotransmitters in our brain to sort and spread, by order of importance, the plethora of information we're thinking throughout our whole body through the releasing of hormones, its intricate messaging system that turns thoughts into actions. Whether your thoughts are predominantly negative or positive, your body (i.e., your nervous system) will always respond accordingly. The same goes with emotions. Emotions and thoughts are closely interconnected. One can easily trigger the other in different scenarios or circumstances to produce the same neurochemicals in the brain. If you're feeling low, try thinking positively. If you find yourself having incessantly negative thoughts, change the narrative as soon as possible by doing something that makes you feel good.

Tapping into emotions goes a long way when manifesting the life of your dreams. One of my favorite things to do to activate my creative power and trigger positive emotions is journaling. Journaling engages your brain in its full capacity by activating the ventrolateral prefrontal cortex, responsible for concentration, planning, prediction, coordination, personal development, adjusting complex behaviors, and setting and achieving goals. There is no right or wrong way to journal.

Don't worry about grammar or neat handwriting. It doesn't need to be aesthetically pleasing. It's reserved for your eyes only. Just get yourself a journal, or for now some paper and a pen, and begin to write.

Having a personal journal to write down your goals, thoughts, feelings, and visualizations is fundamental to achieving greatness. Your journal has to be something that you love contributing to. And why wouldn't you? When you write, you discover yourself at a much deeper level. I've experienced times when I'm feeling off and am not really sure why I'm feeling that way, but as soon as I begin to write in my journal, the answer just comes. Writing has been a monumental part of my healing journey. It's led me to discover myself, be more at ease, gain clarity, give thanks, and ultimately become who I am today. If you love it as much as I do, you can even have separate journals for each writing method. I personally have my gratitude journal, my feelings journal, my goals journal, and my past-tense journal, where I write a fairy-tale story about myself.

My gratitude journal, which is titled *Once Upon a Time*, is where I appreciate everything around me and within me. It's a space where I acknowledge myself for everything I've overcome and acknowledge the support of those around me. It's where I give thanks for the past, even if it was painful, the present moment, and the future yet to come. I've realized that giving thanks is the simplest, easiest route to attracting more of what you want into your life; it brings the positives to the forefront of your mind every day. Gratitude is single-handedly the frequency that flicks the switch from scarcity to abundance.

My feeling journal is where I let out anything significant that I'm experiencing emotionally. It helps me release negative feelings and shift into a better mood. It holds a safe space, free of judgment, comparison, or regret. It's somewhere I can openly write everything I'm thinking and feeling. I normally sign my entries off with, "Now that I've got that out, I am ready to take a step forward into the new me and leave all of this behind."

My goals journal and my past-tense journal come together in one. This is the most powerful journal, one that has helped me gain clarity of my vision and manifest exactly what I want. The first thing I do is close my eyes and picture specifically what I want to achieve. Your brain can't tell if what you are thinking about is real or not (yet). Having a clear vision is fundamental before taking any form of action. Think about every single detail, color, sense, and feeling. Focus on that feeling. How does the manifestation of what you most desire make you feel? What is the energy of that scenario in your head? Really feel it and write it down. After I have my main goal crystal clear, what I do (and I want you to do too) is write three goals that I want to achieve every single day. Every night, before you go to bed, write down three small goals that will act as stepping-stones to achieving your main goal. Then, underneath that, think of three even smaller goals that you can complete right now. And it could be the tiniest thing. For example, they could be journaling, making dinner for your kids, making your bed first thing in the morning, or doing a yoga practice. The completion of those goals begins to accumulate slowly and brings you closer to reaching that huge goal you have, ever-present in the back of your mind.

Smaller goals are much less intimidating, and they provide you an immediate sense of achievement, while also being sustainable in the long run. Just by accomplishing three tiny goals each day, you'll have done 1,095 goals each year that align with your higher purpose. Isn't that amazing? By feeling a sense of achievement, the RAS in your brain will roar "I'm an achiever," and your reality, attention, and sense of what's possible will shift like a magnet toward the manifestation you are affirming.

Right now, pause your reading and write down your main goal along with your three smaller goals for today. Think about how your immediate actions will benefit your life and help you achieve your target. It's equivalent to climbing to the top of a mountain. You have to walk steadily step by step, making each step intentional, and before you know it, you're at the top of the mountain. And the view is so spectacular that any hardships from the climb are already long forgotten.

Within neuroscience, neuroplasticity refers to the brain's process of reprogramming and rewiring, its ability to adapt itself to a specific experience, teaching, or even injury. It is a continuous process that can happen at any time and at any stage in life. When you learn a new skill, your brain quite literally changes and adapts to become more effective and adequate for the specific skill you're developing. The new information you absorb creates new neural pathways. (This is also the reason we've seen humans overcome conditions like ADHD, autism, developmental diseases, and strokes.)

Goal setting, as explained by Dr. Rebecca J. Compton, involves a series of processes that physically restructure and reshape our brain (neuroplasticity) for it to be adequate, optimal, and more effectively wired to reach your desired goal. In technical terms, the process is as follows: "First, emotional significance is evaluated preattentively by a subcortical circuit involving the amygdala; and second, stimuli deemed emotionally significant are given priority in the competition for access to selective attention. This process involves bottom-up inputs from the amygdala as well as top-down influences from frontal lobe regions involved in goal setting and maintaining representations in working memory."[11]

Put simply, your brain adapts in order to keep you focused on achieving the goals that your amygdala (the part of your brain responsible for emotions, memory, and the activation of your fight or flight response) has evaluated and categorized as most important to you.

Now, your most important goal must, of course be your main goal. It should be that one big goal you wrote down, the one all those smaller, daily goals are based on. More than one hundred studies by the American Psychological Association (APA) revealed that specific, challenging goals can lead to better performance and a higher output than easier or vague goals. If your goal is ambiguous, it is the equivalent of having no goal whatsoever. It's also proven that having shorter time limits leads to a more driven working pace than longer time limits, which is why setting a specific time and date for your manifestations is of vital importance. As Elon Musk says, "If you give yourself thirty days to clean your home, it will take you thirty days. But if you give yourself three hours, it will take you three hours. The same applies to your goals, ambitions, and potential."

One study by the APA uncovered the following: "We found that 99 out of 110 studies found that specific, hard goals produced better performance than medium, easy, do-your-best, or no goals. This represents a success rate of 90%." It goes on to say, "Given that goal setting works, it is relevant to ask how it affects task performance. We view goal setting primarily as a motivational mechanism (although cognitive elements are necessarily involved). The concept of motivation is used to explain the direction, amplitude (effort), and duration (persistence) of action. Not surprisingly, all three are affected by goal setting. Most fundamentally, goals direct attention and action."[12]

Achieving a goal is comparable to learning a foreign language. It depends on a series of habits, persistent and aligned action, and thoughts and emotions that will continue to create new neural pathways that allow you to reach your desired goals. Strengthen your mind, your neuroplasticity, and your neurotransmitters. Understanding the science behind the Law of Attraction will help the rational part of your brain implement all the practices and methodologies that I share with you.

The other part of my goals and past-tense journal that I absolutely adore, and that has also been of tremendous help, is writing my own fairy-tale story. I write in past tense and in third person as if this character called Natasha had the life of her dreams and achieved everything she set her mind to. You'll be surprised to learn at this point that this fantasy story has come true. In every aspect, I'm now living my own real-life fairy-tale story.

I always open with, "There once lived a very special girl named Natasha Graziano, and this is her story." Well, actually, the story began with Natasha Grano, and she became Natasha Graziano halfway through! I wrote, "Natasha always overcame any obstacle that came her way, and she knew she was ready to share her life with a handsome and intelligent man. She eventually married the love of her life and went on to grow and scale her business in giant proportions. She wanted to reach hundreds of millions of people, and she found her way, and then everything exploded like the most incredible fireworks display in her career. As she built it, she marketed her programs through her wonderful contacts and friends, and they shared their aligned missions. They built their enchanting databases. And she shared her mission with the world. She was in all the top magazines and fulfilling her mission to help more people. And she did all this by the end of 2021."

And so, of course, I did.

Writing something like this down helps your brain digest it, process it, and believe it to be true, because it's written as if it had already happened. I wrote that in 2020. Remember, by including a specific date and time, you are also manifesting in time and space. That makes you more committed to achieving your goals in that time frame, thus more likely to achieve it overall. If you leave it open-ended, you could end up taking years to manifest any one of your goals.

You can apply neuroplasticity to anything that you want: health, love, wealth, happiness, financial abundance, etc. Napoleon Hill, who I studied the work of for so many years, said, "Whatever the mind can conceive and believe the mind can achieve." That, quite literally, is neuroplasticity.

Modern science has proven that anyone can teach their mind to manifest more effectively, because neuroplasticity means that neurons have the flexibility to create new neural pathways and essentially be trained in a new way of thinking, doing, and being. That's why the neural process is so important for my MBS method. All these teachings combined will make it virtually impossible for you *not* to manifest the life you desire. Evolution starts from within. Everything you desire, you access through your mind, starting as a seed that you water and nurture until eventually it grows into a giant oak tree that even the greatest of storms can't shake. Plant your seed into the garden of your mind, into the womb of your soul. Let that mere thought expand and grow to immense proportions.

There is a quote in the Bible from Matthew 21:22 that says, "If you believe, you will receive whatever you ask for in prayer." This is a verse I personally love because it reminds me that when you pray, not necessarily to any God in particular but sending your intention to the Universe, you tune into a state of gratitude, confidence, and power. By just asking for what you want and need, you are open and ready to receive. So, don't be afraid to ask! Don't wait another minute. You've got nothing to lose and everything to gain. Set your goal, as ambitious as it might seem, and know that your mind and the Universe are working in tandem to make that goal happen.

Synchronicity: Aligning your thought patterns with your feelings and actions to step into heart and brain coherence and deeper alignment.

Heart and brain coherence, properly called psychophysiological coherence, refers to the perfect balance between our psychological (mental and emotional) and our physiological (bodily) aspects. It refers to our thoughts, feelings, desires, and actions coming into resonance, so we can turn into our best selves and become a magnet for abundance. According to HeartMath Institute Director of Research Rollin McCraty, "Psychophysiological coherence is the state of optimal function. Research shows that when we activate this state, our physiological systems function more efficiently, we experience greater emotional stability, and we also have increased mental clarity and improved cognitive function. Simply stated, our body and brain work better, we feel better, and we perform better."[13]

By being in alignment, you can more easily manifest, create, attract, and achieve anything you desire. We have been misled to believe that either the brain controls the heart, or the heart controls the brain, when in reality, the two work together. Both the heart and the brain respond to the other's processes. Thoughts, emotions, and experiences are all elements that affect and influence both the heart *and* the brain; therefore, acknowledgement of both in the manifestation process is crucial. They must work together to evolve as one. When our heart intelligence (our EQ or emotional intelligence) is not aligned with our cognitive processing, it can soon turn into a vicious cycle of disappointment, frustration, and anguish.

Frequencies from the brain are not the only vibrations we emit. Unsurprisingly, the heart projects a powerful electromagnetic field, sixty times greater in force than brain waves. In fact, that can be sensed and measured in an electrocardiography. This electromagnetic field can be expanded up to six feet from a person, and it can project your energy to other people. You have heard people refer to someone's energy as an aura; this is what they are referring to. Having our heart at ease with who we are heavily influences our relationships and our overall performance.

Joseph Murphy, author of *The Power of your Subconscious Mind* writes, "Tune in with infinite intelligence and continue in right thought, right feeling, and right action, and you will arrive at your goal."[14] This is exactly what synchronicity is. You must align your thoughts, your feelings, and your actions together. Once you're in alignment, your actions become inspired by this new combination of thoughts and feelings, and your goal will come to fruition before you even realize it.

Wallace D. Wattles describes in his book, *The Science of Getting Rich*, "There is a thinking stuff from which all things are made, and which, in its original state, permeates, penetrates and fills the interspaces of the Universe. A thought in this substance produces the thing that is imaged by the thought."[15] Your ability to access that higher realm of creation depends on your level of psychophysiological alignment that will pervade your being with a sense of oneness between you and The Universe. We are what we think. We are what we feel. We are what we do. And as a result, we are where we are.

Chapter 5:

Attracting Abundance in Every Area of Your Life

M anifesting all you desire is so much easier than you think. There are a multitude of effective methods, some that I've already shared with you and many I've taught to my clients over the years. All of the methods I share in this book are ones I've personally identified as the most impactful through extensive research, study, and application to my own life.

Joseph Murphy, author of over thirty books, including *The Power of Your Subconscious Mind*, affirms, "God is the source of my supply. His riches flow to me freely, copiously, and abundantly. All my financial and other needs are met at every moment of time and point in space, there is always a divine surplus."[16] Now imagine if you actually lived by those principles. Imagine walking through your life knowing that a higher power—God, the Universe, or whatever you refer to a higher power as—always had your back. Would it make a difference in what you put into action every day? Would you feel any differently toward yourself and others?

Having an unshakeable belief in your limitless potential and the creative powers of the Universe will garner you the freedom to create and manifest the life of your dreams. Have confidence that everything you set your mind to, you will achieve. Picture already being beyond the finish line. Believe it, feel it, own it, and inspire yourself to take immediate action. Why sit back and wait when you have that much power within you to create abundance in every area of your life—in your health, finances, and love life? Once you've mastered the correct mindset and methods, you become unstoppable. Let me show you how.

> *Let me show you how to attract abundance in a key area of your life, your finances. Consider this your pocket guide to manifesting financial miracles.*

It's important for you to understand that anything is possible if you truly, wholeheartedly believe it to be so. You can manifest anything—finances, finding true love, optimal health. It's your birthright to experience a plenitude of abundance in every area of your life.

In my early stages of consciously awakening, I became captivated by the ideas of great philosophers and thought leaders throughout the ages: Eckhart Tolle, Napoleon Hill, Joseph

Murphy, Albert Einstein, and Aristotle, among many others. They helped expand my vision when it came to owning the potential for financial freedom and understanding what my adversity had to teach me. One of my favorite sixteenth-century poets, Rumi, said, "The cure of pain is in the pain." This sentence felt like my personal prophecy. I had to endure a near death experience to discover the path to feeling fully alive—and I wouldn't have changed a thing.

If someone had prophesied what the future held for me when I was bedridden, that I would soon go from broke and homeless to manifesting the life of my dreams, I wouldn't have believed them even for a single second. It never occurred to me that the weakest point of my existence would provide the fuel to light a fire within me, driving me to become the ultimate version of myself and an inspiration and support to millions. After years of studying self-development books, chasing after what I thought would cultivate that magic or breakthrough within me, I found myself down another rabbit hole. My circumstances made me constantly question my capabilities, wondering how I was going to conquer the vast sea of problems I was enduring at the time. I was feeling hopeless and felt the hard thump of rock bottom shake me to my very core. Then, I thought to myself, "If this is the bottom of it all, then the only way to go is up."

Every day, no matter how dark a situation appears, there's always a glimmer of hope—of light—hiding in the corner. It may only be for one second, but if you can find it and focus your attention on that light, allowing yourself to bathe in that energy, you will have the opportunity to follow it, to do something magical with it. You'll be able to shift the narrative of your reality to something that will bring feelings of excitement for what's ahead.

After I experienced that first breakthrough, the epiphany that we are all creators of our own reality became clear to me and I started applying my MBS method across all areas of my life. Once I understood its healing benefits for physical health from my own experience, my belief in its powers only strengthened. I started to apply it with money next. I'd begin by removing any self-limiting beliefs around my finances. Up until this point I was ignorant that I even had any, let alone was I willing to acknowledge they'd be the biggest blocks for me in achieving financial freedom. I remembered that as a little girl I would constantly hear my parents saying, "We don't have enough money. We can't afford a new pair of shoes for school every year. Money doesn't grow on trees." Perhaps some of these statements resonate? Maybe you also faced a strong monetary taboo like this growing up.

The act of going back in time, revisiting your story, and acknowledging where those beliefs stem from begins the unwinding process. Becoming aware of these beliefs allows us to work to remove them.

When I was a child, I loved gymnastics. I'd travel to national competitions representing South England when I was around twelve years old. And I remember all the other children would enjoy their snacks. They had money to use the vending machines, which back then was super exciting for any kid! But I couldn't join in their excitement. I couldn't even afford a chocolate bar. I was embarrassed and ashamed, always feeling like the odd one out. This situation, which to an adult might seem minor, felt monumental for that little girl many years ago. The plethora of emotions from those experiences became lodged in my subconscious, reemerging years later in my adult years as reoccurring money struggles. That struggle did, however, fuel my goals to be abundant, so my family and my children would never have to feel how I felt growing up.

Despite my parents coming into a better financial position later, those monetary pains and traumas had already solidified themselves into my subconscious. I always assumed not having enough, as I heard my parents say, was normal; it was my reality. Experiences that transmute into stored limiting beliefs are particularly potent within our subconscious minds up to the age of about seven, though at the time, of course, we're far too young to realize the massive impact our thoughts and emotions are having on our future selves.

As I explored my limiting beliefs, I soon recognized that I needed to get rid of the financial burdens I'd been carrying for so many years. My beliefs were the main reason why generating the income I needed seemed near impossible. I was barely making enough to cover the essentials each month, like rent and food for my son, with a few pounds in my pocket left to save if I was lucky.

After understanding how the mind works, I understood my vicious cycle of scarcity and lack. Based on the way society, school, and my parents had conditioned me to think, I created my reality based on the only truth I knew, setting the stage for my reality to play out in real time. My own barriers were all that needed to be broken. This rang so true for me once I woke up to the fact that the only limitations we have are the ones we create in our own minds.

When you close your eyes, there's an infinite space of possibilities. Try it out now. Close your eyes. If you really look out in front of you, how far does that blank endless space go on for? It goes on and on and on and on. It's limitless. It's all around you.

Money is no different. It has no bounds; it's infinite.

I had to visit my darkest hour to realize there had to be something more. In this game of life, if I can lose it all, then surely, I can win it all back, right? But how do I do that?

I got it all back by applying the MBS method, by removing all my limiting beliefs, and by getting rid of the things holding me back from achieving more. Then I would continue to work through carefully selecting my new thought processes, refreshingly positive affirmations, and most importantly, aiming for more. Gaining financial abundance (manifesting financial miracles) is based on three key ingredients: self-belief, positively enhanced feelings, and inspired action.

Let's delve deeper into these.

Inspired actions are encouraged by your thought processes, your beliefs, and your goals. This might mean focusing your energy on what will give you bigger and better results, executing those actions, being inspired to knock on more doors, and going after more opportunities. The more doors you knock on, the more chances you'll have, and the more money you'll make. And by doors, I don't always mean knocking in a literal sense. It's more of an analogy for the plethora of possibilities out there, although in the beginning, my first steps actually did involve door-to-door sales.

When I was around eighteen years old, I went around knocking on doors, working in any way I could. I remember working for an agency selling its services to different companies in an area called Oxfordshire near Oxford University in the UK where I grew up. It was an educating field to be in and one in which I acquired the indispensable skill of knowing how to sell to people. When you're face to face with a stranger, if you don't know how to entice their attention by generating the perfect storm of energy in the first few seconds, you won't stand a chance! People will give you around thirty seconds on average, but they've essentially already made their decision in the first five. When I was knocking on physical doors, I realized I could only get through about twenty doors each day, but it always felt like a great day when I could achieve that number.

With the rapid advancement of technology in recent years, birthing a generation of advanced internet gurus, we've created an opportunity to knock on digital doors. Better still, you can knock on way more than twenty doors a day. Let's say you reach out to fifty companies or individuals per day. That's

18,250 digital doors a year! You have already reached tens of thousands of people who are potential new customers and leads! Now that's a tangible way of upping your game and taking huge action toward manifesting more money into your life—all from the tap of a button!

Once you determine what action to take, all it really comes down to is your level of certainty, and this is a crucially important part to focus on. Certainty is believing something is happening. It is trusting that no matter what, something is going to happen; it will come to fruition. It means knowing it is happening for you now and that your goal is already yours. I do that by stepping into the version of me I want to become. Let me share an exercise for you to try right now. All you need is a pen and paper.

Write down what the version of you who you want to become looks like when you are financially abundant, that version of you you've been striving toward. What does that look like for you? What does that feel like? How do you dress now that you are that person? How do you walk, talk, hold yourself? Leave no details out here. Write it all down. Get real clarity on your vision. Know exactly how you'll show up as the ultimate version of you.

When you don't see financial abundance in your life, in your career, in every area of your reality, it's because ultimately, your behaviors do not match those of the person who has already manifested those goals. You aren't yet mirroring the behavior of the person who has already achieved them.

The person who has already achieved your financial vision has an undeniable sense of feeling abundant, like they've got it all. That is the root of misalignment.

Remember, the Law of Attraction is all about aligning yourself to your deepest desires. You must *become* that version of you and, more often than not, that requires change. You can't expect different results by doing the same things you've always done. As Albert Einstein brilliantly puts it, "The purest form of insanity is to leave everything the same and the same time hope that things will change."

If you're feeling a lack of financial abundance in your life, your immediate port of call is to stop worrying about how much things cost every time you pay for something. Flip your energy toward the things you do on a regular basis by focusing on the positive side. For instance, when you receive a bill, instead of having an instantly negative reaction, express gratitude for the service that's been provided. For example, if it is the electricity bill, express gratitude for the electricity provided—for providing water and light to work and earn more money to provide a stable home. Think about all the life enhancements that service has given you.

When you change your outlook on situations like those or when you give to those in need, you embody the vibration of abundance, and it flows in immeasurable quantities. It's a beautiful cycle. Give first, and you shall receive.

It also be that the people you're hanging out with are not serving your purpose. Perhaps they're bringing you down or disrespecting this new version of who you're becoming. Instead of lifting you up, that kind of energy is robbing you of your focus. It's usually not because they don't care for you either; they might believe wholeheartedly that they're acting from a place of love. It's normal for humans to feel fear when facing the unknown, and the protection mechanism to keep you in your comfort zone ensues. Those people might not be the support network you need throughout your transformation.

It's important to surround yourself with people who believe in you wholeheartedly and are willing to be there for you through the good, the bad, and the ugly. You simply don't have the time or the head space for those looking to bring you down with cutting words or even submissively agreeing with everything that comes out of your mouth. It can be equally detrimental to have no one around to call you out. At times, your journey may feel isolating, but if you can stay focused on your goals, you'll end up attracting everyone you need in your life, in the right place, at the perfect time.

If your goal is to have abundant finances, yet you're surrounding yourself with people who lack ambition, curiosity, or an entrepreneurial outlook on life, you're only left with complainers and naysayers. You will get average results in perfect alignment with the average energies you surround yourself with, only leading you farther from your ultimate destination. If, on the other hand, the five people you invest most of your time with are overachievers, successful entrepreneurs who are perhaps well established or taking serious action toward the same sort of financial goals, they will be infectiously ambitious. Surrounding yourself with those who are above average will naturally result in you uplevelling, feeding off their momentum to move forward yourself.

Throughout my journey, I had to cut off so many friends who no longer resonated with me. There is actually a very quick and easy method for you to discover who is a good friend, the kind of person who makes you feel elevated in their presence. I teach this method at many of my talks when I keynote for events. Take a few minutes to complete the worksheet on the next page and, moving forward, reprioritize who you spend time with according to the results.

Self-belief is only possible by becoming aware of the thoughts that create your reality. You can ask yourself: Do I love money? What is my relationship with money? How do I actually feel about money? What's the *why* behind my desire for financial freedom? Because deep down, if you don't actually like money and you believe there is not enough to go around, you are holding onto old-school beliefs like "money is the root of all evil" or "money doesn't grow on trees." In order to grow, you'll need to eradicate those disempowering beliefs rooted inside you. If you don't, you'll carry them with you for years, and I promise you, this is one of, if not, *the biggest reason* why people don't experience the abundance they want in their life. And the worst part? Most people aren't even aware of it!

If you don't believe in money, money will never believe in you. It's mind blowing how intricately our relationship with

Who are the 5 people you spend the most time with? (Write them in order)

1.

2.

3.

4.

5.

What are some qualities you look for in a friend? (Write them in order)

1.

2.

3.

4.

5.

Now score the 5 people you spend the most time with from 0 to 5 on how much they meet each quality you wrote down above.

	Quality 1	Quality 2	Quality 3	Quality 4	Quality 5	TOTAL
1.						/25
2.						/25
3.						/25
4.						/25
5.						/25

*Whoever scored highest is the person you should be spending the most time with money can be connected with our levels of perceived self-worth. You may—consciously or unconsciously—think you don't deserve to have millions of dollars in the bank, that you don't need it, or that it's wrong for you to want that. I regularly hear my clients say before they start working with me say things like "God will love me more for my humble life. People will love me more if I have less. With more money, I'll have more problems." Sound familiar?

All those nonsense lines are made up of the same stuff—limiting beliefs. You want to get rid of those, right? You want to eradicate those voices from your mind so that you can play at a higher level. Say "YES" out loud right now if you do!

The good news is that eradicating limiting beliefs can easily be achieved with an astoundingly simple method. You can say an affirmation every day to start rewiring and hard wiring your new thought processes into your subconscious mind. We want to imprint new beliefs about you and money using affirmations like: "I am worthy of money; I love the things I can do with it."

The more money you have, the more resources and capacity you have; therefore, the more people you can help and the more good you can do in the world. If you want to make your money matter in the world and help people on a big scale, you're never going to be able to make that happen unless you have the means to do so.

Think of every person that is missing out, of every charity that is losing out, because you do not show up at your highest level every day! Think of all those people in your family—

your loved ones, your children, your grandchildren, your great grandchildren-to-be—all those people who would be missing out if you didn't acquire the abundance you were so capable of receiving. You can do so much when you have money, and money is just an energetic by-product of success. The more money you make, the more resources you have, and the more people you can help. Remember that.

The best thing to do when it comes to manifesting financial miracles is to really dig into the reason *why* you want to make the money. What is your driving force? Do you even know what your *why* is? So many people get lost at that first point, yet it's the most important point. I found mine during my darkest time; I had lost my sparkle and was yearning to get my *full light* back. I wanted to be a role model for my son and create the most fulfilling and incredible life for him. Once I'd done that, I wanted to be a role model for hundreds of millions of others around the world, helping them unlock their full potential the same way I did when I tapped into the secret I'm teaching you here in this book.

Look no further to create miracles in your life. It's all right here in your hands. And the best part? You can quite literally manifest financial miracles right here, right now, by following every process step by step. Remember, success in life can only be achieved by taking action.

I'll tell you my even greater *why* that spanned from my first. During my own journey of self-development, it became obvious that when you steer the focus away from yourself—your problems, your issues—and turn your focus toward helping to solve somebody else's problems, your problems subside and seem monumentally smaller. The real abundance really does come down to giving. The law of reciprocity suggests that what you give to others you will then receive from others tenfold.

One day I was at Lakewood Church at a service in Houston, where I was living in my twenties, and the church played a very, very powerful, emotional video of children who were in dire need in Uganda. They were desperate for help, falling short of even basic things like clean water, food, clothes, a roof over their head. The scene brought me to tears. Being presented with this was actually life-changing for me. It highlighted that I had access to all those things, the things so many poor children didn't.

Before I even had my son, I always had this maternal aura, this profound care in my heart for children. Even to this day, hearing a child cry just makes my heart melt, and I want to jump up and do something about it.

After watching the church video, compelled to help in any way I could, I started sponsoring a little girl named Sandrine through the charity the church was representing. I still sponsor her to this day. I look after her, her family, another little boy called Eric, and many of the children and families in their village. My contribution gives them clean water and an opportunity to go to school and have an education. One of my biggest goals for years has been to build an orphanage, and we are well on our way to making this mission materialize. In fact, by the time you read this book, it might have already been built. But until my orphanage is built, I'll continue to make an impact in any way I can.

So, what is abundance really? Abundance is living a life of joy, living exciting experiences, and creating a fulfilled life from which you are able to give back to the world.

Yes, you should have all of life's riches. You are deserving of all of it. You're meant to have everything you've ever dreamed of—and more. It's your birthright to experience all the most beautiful things this life has to offer you, though there's always room to give back. Never forget that part. Giving back creates the most powerful vibration within you, so powerful it's somewhat indescribable. I regained my purpose in giving back, and so I kept doing it. That's what I focused on. That became my *why*. Sandrine and her village became my *why*. It breaks my heart to think that other children are left out there who don't have access to that kind of support. And not only children but also plenty of adults who could use support through a plethora of amazing charities out there. People need more medical resources and there are environmental and climate foundations out there desperate for someone like you to give a helping hand through any form of financial contribution. When you find your calling, your *why*, connect your purpose to your business. Connect your why, and everything you do will make sense, every action you take will be purposeful.

> *When your why is bigger than anything*
> *in your way, you are unstoppable.*

So, what is your *why*? Take some time now to write it down.

Once I connected my *why*, once I connected my purpose to everything I did, the path forward became clear. I went from being a broke single mom to making my first million dollars in less than a year.

The reason why I constantly bring this up is to make you aware that you can achieve this too. I'm not special. You can build it all and create something incredible. I mean, come on; if I could do it, you can do it. I had nothing—no silver spoon, no handout or jumpstart. If I could come out from under the rock I'd been hiding under for years, you can too. With more resources, you can reach more people, and the more people you reach, the greater positive impact you can have on this world.

The women who read this book and implement what I'm sharing will inspire other women to do more with their lives too. They will realize that their purpose is not limited to what society has led them to believe: that our ambitions only go as far as the title of mother or wife or the job our parents expected us to do. That's not true. Your purpose is whatever feels true to you, whatever ignites that fire in your heart, that thing you have such a passion for that you can't bear to go a day without doing something toward it. *That* is your purpose.

Men, too, holding the potential of this work in their hands, will want to implement this knowledge, knowing that when they connect their purpose to their business, they become an inspiration to others in the world. You become superior, an alpha male, stepping up to be the man you were born to be.

And you do that not as the lonely businessman who makes loads of money to just look at. There are too many of those already. Anyone can do that. What are you doing that's different? How are you committing to your life's mission each and every day? I actually believe I can change the world, and I know, step by step, you can too. With commitment and consistency, we can all change the world together.

Your Health: Attracting the Health You Are Meant to Have

As cliché as it sounds, your body really is your temple. If you can master your health, you'll gain the energy, mental clarity, and agility necessary to overcome any obstacle that comes your way. In good health, you can climb the highest mountains.

There are many factors that contribute to having a healthy lifestyle. Some people believe that "looking healthy" translates into ultimate health across the board. In reality, this couldn't be further from the truth. Health, in all its glory, spans across our habits, diet, sleep, activity, and mental well-being, all factors being equally important to conquer.

We've already discussed the importance of cultivating the mindset to feed your mind with all the right things. But when it comes to your health overall, committing to uplevelling the amount of nutrients you're fueling yourself with can have a massive impact. According to the World Health Organization, having a healthy diet "protects you against many chronic noncommunicable diseases, such as heart disease, diabetes and cancer."[17] A healthy, balanced diet also contributes greatly to your brain's ability to function properly, feeding your productivity, your creativity, and your ability to understand information and process it with precision and accuracy.

Eating nutrient-dense food also contributes to the optimal functioning of so many bodily systems. Throughout the modern world, negative eating habits and disorders like anorexia have become normalized in our society—orthorexia, exercise addiction, negative self-talk, compulsive and impulsive behaviors, etc. The idea that our physical appearance is more important than our actual health and well-being is a product of the diet culture of the modern world, and it poses some seriously negative implications for our mental health. The great dissatisfaction that people have with their own appearances, to the point where they believe they have to warp their photos to fit some unachievable ideological norm, just shows the sheer power social media has to impact our mental health. When our mental health is disrupted, attention to our physical health can rapidly spiral too. That is why our mental stability is profoundly important, alongside an understanding that overall health should always be prioritized before aesthetics. Healthy and nutritious food provides clarity for your brain's development and will also facilitate motivation when it comes to fitness. In contrast, when you feed your body nothing but refined sugar, processed foods, highly saturated fats, and empty calories, your body's only response will be to diminish its functioning. If you want to reach your full potential, provide your body and mind with the foundations to work at their best. Be it nutrition, fitness, or mindfulness, you have to step up and do the work.

Be careful not to abuse your body or deprive it from food or sleep. The vessel that is your body already does so much for you. Imagine where it could take you if you treated it right. Work out, exercise your heart muscle (which as you now know is equally important as your brain for manifesting your desires), stretch, strengthen your body, and treat yourself with all the love and abundance you deserve.

When it comes to sleep, many adults mistakenly believe that sleeping for long periods of time is reserved for children, that getting rejuvenating, deep rest is a thing of the past. Having sustainable sleeping habits can change your life. Sleep deprivation is a really serious thing. As neuroscientist Matthew Walker explains, "Sleep loss will leak down into every nook and cranny of your physiology. Sleep, unfortunately, is not an optional lifestyle luxury. Sleep is a nonnegotiable biological necessity. It is your life support system."[18] If you have improper sleeping habits, your intelligence suffers, your memory falters, and you lose the ability to learn new information. You also become more susceptible to illnesses like dementia, strokes, and heart attacks. Your whole immune system weakens, so you're less able to fight off any form of disease or illness. Without adequate sleep, you'll also find that your body hurts more. "Lack of sleep distorts your genes, and increases your risk of death generally," Walker says, "It disrupts the creation of sex hormones like estrogen and testosterone, and leads to premature aging."[19]

Prioritize your eight-hour-long sleep every single night. I know I do. And it makes every day so much brighter, lighter, and more productive. Go to bed at a reasonable hour, free of screens, sounds, or lights, and create a resting space so sacred that it's only function is in helping you relax, rest, and unwind. Understand that sleeping is the source from which your body, your mind, and your creative power operates, and without it, you'll diminish any chance of becoming your best self.

When I had hyperthyroidism, an autoimmune disease, it turned into a downward spiral for me. The more I focused on the pain, the more the pain intensified. The more I focused on my anxiety, the worse the world looked. My physical health was failing, and my mental health was derailing close behind. It just got to a point where I felt I couldn't do it anymore. I'd lost all sense of myself and of everything around me. The saddest part was feeling my identity fade and my purpose in life disintegrate. When you reach rock bottom, you must keep hold of the understanding that the only direction left to go is up. At that moment, the last glimpse of light I had left revealed a piece of golden wisdom. I knew that if I gave up, I would be giving up my faith, and I wouldn't be able to be the best I could be for my son. I remember thinking, "If I give up now, I am never going to have the opportunity to see where mine or my son's life could have gone if I hadn't given up."

When a woman is giving birth naturally, just before she is about to push the baby out, she gets to this point. It happened to me when I was birthing my son, Rio. I was pushing so hard and was in so much pain that I just got to a point where I said, "I can't do this anymore." I remember vividly how I stopped, battling to catch my breath, and I told the doctor, "Please, just take him out another way. I can't do this anymore."

The midwife leaned in and whispered softly in my ear, "Natasha, that's how you know you're near the end. Now is when you are about to give birth to your son, so push as hard as you can right now."

And with tears in my eyes, I did. I pushed two more excruciating times and out came my son.

Scientifically, we call this state transition. Transition is that moment where you are about to break through, yet it feels so difficult and impossible that all you want to do is give in . . . but you keep on moving, and it's that one last push that gets you to the other side. That birth story serves as a great metaphor for life, because when you face a situation so challenging you feel you can't possibly move another step forward, it's indicative of the breaking point where you either push and reach that goal or stay stuck. Always go a little further, push yourself a little harder, and know that your manifestation is waiting right there in front of you.

Disease, illness, and pain—be it physical, emotional, mental, or spiritual—comes to teach us life-changing lessons about ourselves and show us the specific aspects that need more work to heal. So, if and when you notice something is physically wrong, dare to look a little deeper. What is your body trying to communicate to you?

When I had eczema, an autoimmune skin disease, it was really severe and covered my entire body. Everyone in my family had it at some point, so doctors assumed it was genetic. I was recommended all sorts of creams, soaps, and diets. I even remember limiting showers so water wouldn't worsen my condition. And in truth, I did find some relief in those things. But it was like a band-aid masking my symptoms; my disease never left my body entirely. I needed to get down to the root.

I looked within myself and decided to speak directly to my disease, "You don't serve me anymore. Thank you for teaching me what I needed to learn; you can go now. Eczema, leave my body; you are no longer a part of me." I knew the power of the mind, and I trusted those words would heal me. Within a week, the redness, soreness, itchiness, and discomfort disappeared. I remember thinking, "Wow, this is really powerful. You *can* control your outer state through the power of your mind."

We're all capable of generating physical changes in our bodies through thoughts and emotion alone. So, visualize your body healthy, fit, and strong; heal yourself from the power you have within.

One of my clients from LA suffered an accident that made her unable to walk. She was told by doctors that the ligament she tore in her legs would never attach back to the muscle, that she'd never walk again. Despite the lifetime sentence she was given, she applied my MBS method daily and healed herself despite every doctor's expectation.

A similar case happened in Arizona. A man reached out to me because he had recently been diagnosed with premature dementia, which was, again, according to doctors, irreversible and progressive. With nothing to lose, he decided to give my MBS method a try, receiving personal guidance from me. He was consistent and committed, despite on occasion completely forgetting what he'd done the day before. Either way, he stuck to the program, rewired his mind, reprogramed his body, and recalled his former self back into existence. It's been three years now, and his mind is working like never before. Doctors were stunned to see him improving day after day, proclaiming it as a miracle.

Optimizing your health depends on a series of things individual to your unique physiology, but you can, without a shadow of a doubt, heal yourself from illness, disease, and disorders. You can head toward your best life because you deserve to be in perfect health. Acknowledge your body, give thanks for the ability to do the things you do, and treat both your body and your mind with love. Nurture both your body and your mind as you would nurture a child and they will work harmoniously to create your best life and achieve greatness.

Manifesting Love: The Love Attraction Quotient

Most humans share one burning desire: to experience true love. Love, after all, is one of the main reasons we are even here on this earth. Helping people in this area of their lives brings me so much joy. The vibration of love is one of the most powerful on the planet, yet feeling unworthy of it or frustrated with not having it can create a vibrational lack that holds the potential to seep into every other area of your life.

When it comes to manifesting love, just like everything else, it's essential to be clear on your vision and align yourself with the person you want to attract. I'm going to give you three powerful techniques that will build your confidence and self-empowerment to make you feel worthy of your soul mate or help strengthen your current relationship. I'm humbled to say I've helped many people manifest their soul mate with the three tools I'm about to share with you, so make sure you fully commit to the practices, fully trusting that love can and will happen for you as it did for me and so many others.

Not too long ago I manifested the love of my life, my husband, using these very tools within just three weeks of setting my intention to the Universe. We got married after three months. Manifesting love into my life has come naturally to me over the years; I attract partners who match the version of myself at that moment in time. As Wayne Dyer wisely says, "You don't get what you want. You get what you are." This is the foundation of what I teach you, so you can manifest love that makes you feel alive and actually keep it once you've attracted it.

The first step I encourage you to take is to write down a list of one hundred things about your dream partner. What does he or she look like? How does he or she make you feel? What are their best qualities? Their strengths and weaknesses? Their likes and dislikes? Be as detailed and clear as you possibly can. The reason why you want to do this is because it makes your ideas tangible—something you can see, sense, and touch—outlining what you really want. Take your time filling out the list; it's an essential element and a solid foundation for our next steps. To make it easier, you can break it down into smaller lists under subtitles like character traits, what they like to do in their spare time, how they look, feel, smell, etc.

Once you have completed this list, it's time to move on to part two. I want you to ask yourself the following question: From what I have written, on a scale from 1 to 10, how am I showing up as the person I've described? If you want to manifest a dream partner who embodies all those attributes, you have to first *become* that person. You must reflect all those gorgeous qualities of your future soul mate to attract that same energy into your reality. If you are less than an 8/10 in any of the characteristics or personality traits that you're seeking, that is the work you need to do to attract that level of partner to you. You must *Be It Until You Become It.* Become the kind of person you want to marry.

If you are coming from a needy mindset of wanting to see what you can get from a partner, then you will ultimately end up with a partner who repeatedly takes from you. But if you are going into a relationship with a giving mindset, you will always be rewarded with a generous partner.

So many people come to me asking why they keep attracting jerks as partners, only to realize they're manifesting someone to fill a gaping hole in their life. They have a fixed fairy-tale image of someone they will one day marry and spend years chasing ideas of how they think their partner should be, utterly oblivious they're shoving the wrong foot into the glass slipper in the first place. Living someone else's fairy tale will never work. The right someone is out there for everyone, and once you step into the best version of you, you'll attract them into your life like a magnet. But until you understand what the Universe is trying to teach you, you continue copying and pasting the same kind of partner wearing slightly different clothes into your life. You have to recognize that they are just a mirror image of yourself. All the traits you don't like are simply a reflection of something you need to work on. The Universe comes to test you too, waiting for the day you finally say no to unacceptable behaviors you usually casually brush aside in a partner. Once you break that cycle, you'll create so much beautiful space to receive the right person into your life.

The final piece of the puzzle, and the third step to manifesting love into your life, is to visualize being in that relationship with your dream person every day. Try sitting quietly every morning and visualizing what it feels like to be married to your soul mate in a healthy, harmonious, and loving relationship. Repeat this ritual before you go to sleep. I like to do it every morning with my cup of manifestation tea. I would open my box of strongly scented tea, indulging my senses in all the magical flavors before I even put it into my cup. I'd visualize being married to my husband and literally feel his arms around me, smiling at our embrace. Then I would sip the tea. I was connecting all five senses to this visualization. This is such a powerful part of this practice because you're triggering different parts of the brain. You are bathing all five senses in this scenario you are imagining, allowing your brain to store it as an actual memory. It doesn't know whether it has happened or not. I do this visualization for a minimum of seventeen seconds every day from anywhere between three and nine times per day.

My bonus tip for you (because this is one of my favorite topics and it just makes my heart smile when people find their soul mates) is to take immediate action to become that person you would want your dream partner to see you as! Wear clothes that make you feel great, take care of your body, eat clean and healthy foods, and exercise your beautiful body. And remember, it's not all about aesthetics; the energy you emanate will aid in your ability to attract. Contrary to popular belief, attraction isn't just physical; it actually has much more to do with energy. One thing that is a bit unconventional but really works is to do a nude photoshoot for yourself. It may sound crazy, and it can be awkward at first, but when you appreciate who and what you are, loving every part of you, that's a great action to take toward who you want to become. Your whole reality will start shifting.

A client, and now friend, of mine named Maria had been in my presence for less than twenty-four hours when she met her soul mate. I was speaking at an event in Las Vegas to thousands of people. I sat with her for an hour, really pouring onto her the power of gratitude, love, and feeling empowered. She told me how she had been single for three years and had really struggled to find a partner who had the qualities to make it long-term. I gave her some of my favorite strategies and techniques, exactly the ones that I'm sharing with you, on how to attract her soul mate, and then I told her, "In fact, your soulmate may even be at this event amongst these thousands of people! Imagine what the chances are that you've come to this event to meet me, finally in person, after having been through so many of my programs for other areas of your life like business, but actually, you just needed to hear these words I'm giving you now." And it triggered something in her like a light switch. I watched her whole body light up with the same glow you'd expect from a newly engaged bride-to-be! It was no surprise when the very next day she did indeed meet her soul mate at that very event. I was even there to witness the moment the two of them actually met, and let me tell you, the chemistry was powerful. It was as if they were looking into each other's souls, and it was a blessing to witness. Today, they're in a happy relationship, living together and soon to be married. Maria is one of many beautiful souls who I've had the pleasure of meeting and playing a part in her becoming a magnet to the love of her life.

As in other areas, the MBS method can remove any limiting beliefs you might have around love. It's important to evaluate your story, the movie script you're writing about your life. Again, assess the things that might have triggered you as a child and heal them in the same way as your finances and health. It's the same process for anything you want to manifest.

When it comes to love, do you know how to receive it? Receiving your manifestations from the Universe is key in this process. Even if you do all the other steps perfectly, if you don't act when the opportunity is in front of you, then how could it ever fully materialize? By knowing your worth, your value, you won't settle for anything less than spectacular. Step one will help you determine which opportunities or people are for you, the situations you tolerate and the ones you shut down for good.

When I first met my husband, it wasn't even in person. He was in Canada, and I was in the United Kingdom. We were speaking online every day for weeks, and one Sunday morning, he showed up on the phone hungover. I sensed his energy and told him, "I'm going to hang up the phone now."

He said sarcastically, "I feel really crap. Thank you for being so sympathetic with me."

I immediately responded, "I am not one of those b**ches who sits on the phone and says, 'Oh sweetie, I'm so sorry! Let me send you a food delivery to help you nurse your hangover.' No! You are going to sit the f down, so the man behind you can stand up if you're not ready to be a superior man. There's always someone right behind you. Unless you're ready to leave these addictive behaviors behind, or whatever it is that you are doing on Saturday nights, and you are ready to put everything else to bed and be the superior man that I need you to be, not only for me, but also for the world, then I'm ready to marry you. Then you can come into my life. But until then, ciao!"

He landed in the UK twenty-four hours later and asked me to marry him. We flew back together to Canada where a few weeks later we had a fairy-tale wedding, covered by the *New York Times*. You can see it all there online if you want to see pictures; it's magical! The reason I share this is because when you tap into that confidence, the right person will come to you; they'll do everything to show you they are worthy of your love.

I even helped my mother manifest her husband. Years ago, after her divorce, she always used to moan, "I'll never meet anyone. I have five children and four of them still live at home. Who would want someone older like me? Who would want to take on all this?" I encouraged her to dare to go on a dating site and equipped her with empowering affirmations to listen to every morning, the same ones I give my clients in my Manifest Love Programs, to build her self-love and confidence. We also did an earlier form of my MBS method together to remove her limiting beliefs and love blockages, and now, my mother is happily married, and it fills me with so much joy seeing her happy, living out the life she always wanted.

If you throw yourself into these practices wholeheartedly, no circumstance or situation can stand in your way of manifesting love. It's all right there, in your mind and your heart. It's about creating space to be able to receive and believing you're worthy of love—because you are. We all are. That's why we are here, isn't it? To experience love in all its magnificent forms.

Another crazy beautiful story of two souls who came together through my method is a couple who met on one of my weekly conference calls for Law of Attraction Secrets. This was the same place I met my husband. The two of them were so inspired by my story with Michael that they continued to attend our room for almost a year every Sunday where they used my methods to manifest each other. Their determination clearly paid off as they too are now happily married and continuing to inspire singletons and show them that attracting love is possible without even having to meet someone in person. These two are just another example of hundreds of couples I have helped manifest love. Some say once they've been in my presence, be it in person or online, something unlocks within them. I always assure them it's not me doing it. I'm simply holding space and providing the tools to unlock that key within themselves to manifest anything they desire. Falling in love with *who you are* by being the best you can be is the key to attracting a like-minded soul into your life, and I've fallen utterly in love with helping people become a manifestation magnet for the one who sets their soul on fire.

Chapter 6:

The Five Pillars
of Achieving Your Goals

When we find the perfect recipe for a meal and it
tastes absolutely exquisite, the next time we cook
it, we aim to mimic those exact same steps with
the delicious outcome in mind. It took me years of studying,
practicing, and research to uncover the perfect recipe for manifestation. Now, after copious trial and error, I have refined the
steps to manifest anything and everything you desire. I call
them The Five Pillars of Manifestation. The five pillars bring
you face to face with who you want to be and what you want to
do in this world to seriously upgrade your life—and ultimately
fulfill your soul's purpose.

Pillar One: Get Clarity of Your Vision
One of the biggest problems from the get-go is not knowing
what you want. We all face this at some point in our life.

You'd think answering "What do I want?" would be a simple process, but the question often strikes a chord and invites you to look deeper.

As I mentioned earlier, we've *all* been conditioned in one way or another, often to the point where our aspirations turn toward fulfilling the roles and expectations people have of us before ever considering the expectations we've laid out for ourselves. What I encourage you to realize here is that to become more than just an idea your parents laid out for you, you have to believe in your limitless capacity to achieve. If you *believe* you can achieve, your vision will always head in the direction of greatness. Better still, by applying the MBS method, you'll get crystal clear on the *why* behind your vision, allowing you to effectively uproot and eliminate any self-limitations that might cause delays on the way to your ultimate destination.

Getting clarity of your vision goes a lot further than just thinking about who you want to be. You need to physically embody it to activate your powers of creation, making those ideas and dreams that ignite your soul a reality. I'll never stop reiterating the power of writing your vision down, so let's do it. Start by answering the following questions:

- What's behind your aspirations? Why do you feel called to pursue them?
- Who do you want to be? What version of yourself will make your dream a reality?

- How are you going to make it happen? What do you want to manifest into your life?
- How does your dream benefit others? How does it serve the world? How will it serve the world once you're gone? Could your goal continue to flourish? What does that look like?

Write your answers down with so much detail and clarity that you feel the energy rushing through you. The stronger the emotional connection, the higher the vibration propelling you to live out your purpose. You can make it a paragraph, as Napoleon Hill wrote in his 1937 book, *Think and Grow Rich*, "Read your statement aloud, twice daily, one just before retiring at night, and one after you rise in the morning. As you read, make sure to see and feel your statement and believe yourself into possession of your desires."[20]

Your statement will likely change and evolve over time. Three months from now, your goals may shift completely, or perhaps you'll have already attained some of the things you wrote by then. The beauty of the knowledge you're receiving in this book is that you'll be able to repeat the process to achieve bigger and bigger goals moving forward, implementing skills that stay with you for a lifetime.

There's a powerful breathing technique I like to use to intensify the effects of this step. The importance of breath is applicable everywhere. Nasal breathing and humming increase production of nitric oxide in your body; known as a bronchodilator, it widens the arteries, decreases blood pressure, and invigorates the body, increasing blood flow to tissues, muscles, cells, and organs, which creates a supersonic thinking haven! If you want to enhance your quality of mind and work effectively in an optimal state, increasing levels of nitric oxide in your body is the perfect place to start.

Another way to achieve this is through a great practice called "box breathing," often utilized by the military for its ability to quickly initiate a flow state, that perfect balance of energized calm. It's super simple too. You inhale for four seconds, hold your breath for four seconds, exhale for four seconds, and then hold the breath for another four seconds, repeating the cycle over and over. It's worth noting the importance of relaxing into your body here. If you're working from a place of tension, you won't reap the benefits.

When you're in a heightened state of awareness like those that come from breathing techniques, you're able to receive streams of downloads from the Universe, defining and creating all your objectives for anything you want to accomplish.

The next thing you want to do, just as Napoleon Hill mentioned, is repeat your statement often and consistently to enhance its power, creating a morning and evening ritual around it. These two moments of your day are really powerful. They are your brain's prime time to produce theta waves, which correspond to intuitive, visionary, and creative levels of experience—right before you go to sleep and as soon as you wake up. It's a perfect state to set your intentions, so they are embedded into your subconscious mind, setting you up for autopilot manifestation for the rest of the day. Be sure to stay away from electronics at this time. This is your space; everything else can wait.

Repeat your statement loud and clear. Make it special; it's likely the most important part of your day. You can also use this time to do things that make you feel amazing, like doing yoga, meditating, reading books that inspire you, or having a special cup of tea. Make it memorable. Doing so will show the Universe your unwavering loyalty to this goal—and yourself.

Gratitude is possibly the most powerful frequency to wake up to. Before doing anything else, I'd encourage you to, as soon as you wake up, to say, "Thank you, thank you, thank you for this day." Indulging in that feeling of gratitude sets the tone for the day ahead. Place your feet on the ground and be grateful for everything around you, voicing affirmations like, "Thank you for the abundance in my life. Thank you for my bed, for my duvet, for my sheets. Thank you for my healthy body, for the people I have in my life, my family, my loved ones . . ." Express gratitude for every single thing you can think of.

Post gratitude, read your statement out loud. Repeat it as many times as it takes to tap into the emotions of already being there. It has to feel real to you; that's where the power of your practice resides. Finally, do your practice, whichever one helps you raise your vibration and makes you feel your best. Movement is the best form of medicine to emit a flow of energy throughout your body; it's also great for your overall health.

Remember, astounding results are only possible through commitment to these rituals every day. Only form habits that will bring out the best in you.

It's because of my daily rituals that I now live the life I always dreamed of, and repeating them helps me achieve new goals time and time again. Upon waking, as soon as I open my eyes, I say "Thank you for giving me another day, thank you for my heartbeat, for my breath. Thank you, husband, for lying next to me and always taking care of me. Thank you for your guidance." I repeat these words of gratitude and then I follow with my statement out loud. By now, I know it by heart, and you will too in time. Until then, you can write it down on a post-it note and pin it somewhere visible to you throughout your day.

Next, I meditate. I connect with Source, with Light, with God, the Universe, however you want to name it. Feeling connected with this higher energy and aligned with your purpose will guide your every action, every step, every thought with what you came here to accomplish. In meditation, I'll often ask for guidance, asking the Universe to reveal the steps I can take today. I always ask the same question: "How can I better serve people? How can I serve *more* people?"

You'll soon realize that the ultimate goal is always defined by a purpose beyond yourself. When you intend on serving others, the Universe will instantly provide you with everything you need—and more. You'll miraculously come across all the right people, circumstances, "coincidental" encounters, signs . . . they will all appear as if by magic.

I learned the hard way about the backlash you get from manifesting things for your sole benefit. Sure, they might bring a momentary glimpse of joy, but it fades as soon as it comes. The need for more only gets stronger; the gaping hole within widens. In the past, I often wanted things for selfish reasons. Even if I did experience abundance, sometimes in enormous quantities, as though a rug was literally ripped from underneath my feet, it all vanished moments after receiving it. If what you do has no benefit to the lives of others, then it's not your true calling. It might benefit you in the short term, but it's not serving a wider purpose. Only when I shifted my life to one of service did I feel purposeful, and unsurprisingly, everything started happening with ease. Now my mission has evolved to better serve humanity long after I've departed this earth, to create a legacy that continuously benefits the wider collective.

The only way to learn how to be of service to others is by manifesting from a place of love, compassion, and positivity, removing your ego from the picture completely. That's the ultimate difference between authentic manifestation and manifesting for only your benefit. Bear this principle in mind when you're creating your statement and envisioning your goals and it will happen.

Pillar Two: Remove the Blockages

By now, removing limiting beliefs and reprogramming your mind should be familiar concepts. Naturally, as you move closer to your goals, different blockages will arise along the way. Luckily, with the techniques we've covered, you now possess an inherent ability to detach with the full awareness that you are not your beliefs and overcome them. When I first started teaching the MBS method to clients, or sometimes thousands of people at a time at live events, common phrases fed back to me would be things like: "It's like three years of therapy in fifteen minutes! I've never been able to shift this pain I've had with me until I understood how to remove it using the MBS method."

One incredibly touching story is about a lady named Jennifer, who I met a few years ago at one of my in-person masterminds. I started with a powerful forgiveness exercise to release anything they needed to let go of before we could start the week's work. I asked the group to forgive someone for something they had been holding onto and, in turn, forgive themselves. Jennifer came to me an hour after the exercise and asked if we could talk privately for a moment. She told me how she and her mother had always had a really horrible relationship; they hadn't spoken for the past twenty years. They'd tried therapy three times across the years, but she told me she'd given up hope and lost all faith that her mother would ever change. Therapy helped Jennifer understand that her mother had projected all of her own anger onto her daughter from a really young age, describing the environment she grew up in as hostile, resulting in the development of deep-rooted traumas and issues spanning well into her adult life. Jennifer was forty-five when I met her. Even after all that time, she didn't realize the sheer grip her heavy limiting beliefs had on her. Within five minutes of doing the exercise, she told me she'd gotten a text from her mother saying, "Jennifer, this is your mother. I don't know why I felt to ask you to call me, but something told me that I needed to call you today. If you can find it in your heart, please give me a ring." Jennifer phoned straight away and had the most beautiful phone call she had ever had with her mother in her entire lifetime. Jennifer said it was like speaking to a different person, the words rolling off her own tongue differing from their usual tones and styles. She experienced a feeling of lightness, a letting go of the past and all that happened between them, leaving only a sense of unconditional love for her mother. And what's more, her mother reciprocated. Jennifer thanked me profusely. I assured her it wasn't me who had healed her relationship. The method had simply facilitated a space for Jennifer to learn how to heal her heart. Miracles do happen. In the words of Michael Jackson, start with the man in the mirror.

The following exercise is a practical method to help you discover what could be blocking you.

Make a two-column grid on a piece of paper. In the first column, write the title "A Negative Energy that I Want to Eradicate." Think about what that disempowering voice is telling you, that devilish fiend who pops up, trying to stop you from achieving miracles, doing everything in its power to prevent you believing that you can. What is stopping you right now? Remember, the "X" on your map is inside of you. The feeling, that belief, that is blocking you is rooted within you.

Column two is titled "My Life Now Without the Problem." Here you describe how, if that limitation wasn't there, you would think, feel, speak, and act. Imagine your life now without that limiting belief bombarding your experience. What does that look like? How does it feel? Imagine you're telling a friend. Tell them. Explain it. Indulge in all that emotion and write it down in detail. There's something about putting pen to paper that's pure magic. It creates a sense of it actually coming to fruition in your mind and works to manifest it.

Pillar Three: Anchoring Your New Belief System

I'd like you to start anchoring your new belief system by doing a simple exercise. Write down how you can transcend your negative energy to a more positive one and note who else it serves as you're playing out this new reality. It might sound something like this: "If I let go of the grudge I'm holding against (fill in the blank), I'm then able to exchange that negative energy for positive vibrations, feel great about myself, and attract a new outcome. My perspective will shift, and new opportunities will flow into my life. Now, I'm abundantly wealthy. I'm more able to help others. I could open a charity, give to my family, and help my loved ones." Gaining access to an altered state of awareness is the simplest way of anchoring your new belief system. You can do this through meditations, NLP, or any other form of deep mind work like my MBS meditations, where we reprogram our mind from the roots, visualizing the result while tuning into our highest frequencies for manifestation.

Rewiring your subconscious mind and hard wiring your new belief system is the act of choosing which thoughts and feelings you allow into your mind. Should you find yourself having an old limiting belief, not feeling worthy, or feeling lesser, immediately stop the thought in its tracks and tell it to go away! Then replace that negative limiting belief with its exact opposite.

Let's put this into context. You start to think, "I'm not as good as her. Why does *she* have that and I don't?" Then you'd stop that narrative in its tracks and flip it instantly to something along the lines of, "I *am* good enough. I can't compare myself to others. I'm so happy that she has those things, because it inspires me to know if she can do it, I can too." You can even integrate methods like tapping; you tap where in your body you feel the limiting belief is stored, and you say, "I release this limiting belief!" You then tap the other side of your body to imprint your new positive belief with an aligned affirmation.

Pillar Four: Expand Your Vision

Pillar four is one of my favorites. It's all about using your imagination. When I became a mother, I watched my son growing every day, playing in the garden with his toys. He used his imagination in the most incredible way, as children so often do. They can visualize the Universe at their fingertips, opening the door to seeing anything they want. He'd tell me about the fairies and a great spectrum of things he could see. He'd play games with imaginary friends, which is particularly magnificent because children haven't yet learned to tell the difference between imagination and reality. Their minds are so present and powerful. Of course, over the years, society, school, and other people's values infiltrate them, and that excitement for life steadily drains. I want to show you how to regain that excitement, that curiosity for the world.

The most immediate course of action is a vision board. I first heard about vision around fifteen years ago from my dear friend John Assaraf in the film, *The Secret*. When I first heard John's words, first in the book and later in the movie, it clicked. Imagining your life into existence wasn't silly or childish at all; it was genius. I realized I could design my life like an architect and use this as a tool to attract anything I dreamed of into my reality. I never imagined that years later I'd be manifesting *him*, along with other idols, from my vision board into my life as friends and work colleagues. What's even more astounding is that when I recently went to surprise a client of mine in person at her home in Los Angeles, as soon as we walked in with the film crew, she burst into tears and said, "I can't believe I'm *actually getting this opportunity* to meet you in person! I wrote three years ago in my journal that one of the things I wanted to manifest in my life was meeting Natasha and being mentored by her in person. I stuck an image of you on stage on my vision board, and here you are now!" She went on to tell me that she had used my MBS method to manifest that moment, showing me all the things on her vision board that had come to fruition since being mentored by me, thanking me for the tools that helped her understand how to use the power of her subconscious mind and make those ideas a reality. Just like she did, you can too.

Vision boards are satisfying to create physically using arts and crafts methods, or you can also create one digitally. I made my first vision board in my late teens with magazine cut-outs. I remember writing affirmative beliefs next to each image about what I wanted most in my life. A top tip for how to get excited by your vision board is to print multiple images of things that inspire you, things you want to experience, places you want to see in your lifetime. I've been creating them for nearly two decades now and enjoy redoing them annually. Renewing it regularly strengthens my belief system and looking back at each board realizing I've manifested everything on them never gets old. That sense of achievement amplifies your drive to *Be It Until You Become It.*

> *"For me, becoming isn't about arriving somewhere or achieving a certain aim. I see it instead as forward motion, a means of evolving, a way to reach continuously towards a better self. The journey doesn't end." —Michelle Obama*

Think about how you'd like every single area of your life to look: your love life, your business, your finances, your family life, your philanthropic work. Bring to your mind that which brings you immense joy, play your favorite music, really indulge in this new you.

I love that word—indulge. It actually plays a part in being it until you become it. Forget fake it 'till you make it; be it until you become it. Really take that in. Dedicate that time to yourself. Take a couple of hours for yourself, get lost in the rhythm of your music as you go along, enjoy it, indulge! Feel that future version of yourself. What do you feel like? What do you look like? What does the environment you've created look like? Focus on that. What does it feel like now that you have achieved these goals?

The other day, I got a little nostalgic and pulled out one of my old vision boards from seven years ago. I was stunned. I'd literally manifested every single thing on that page to the last detail—the cars, the homes, the dream partner, my child, the love and abundance, the eight-figure business. Now, a word of caution. Any detail you miss, the Universe will fill in for you, so do not miss details. Imagine buying something online, scouring the internet until you find that thing you love the most before finally placing your order, so you can go about the rest of your day. Let's say you were looking for a new suit, for example. You'd start imagining how great it's going to look on you and when you find that one perfect fit, you place your order and voila! It arrives on your doorstep. You even select the date that you want it to arrive by. Now, assuming you fall into the category of most people in this context, you don't usually call the company and ask, "Hey, who's delivering it to me? Which driver is delivering it? What car is he driving?" Of course not! You automatically trust that it's going to be delivered as promised. The same applies to your vision board! You put your order into the Universe, stating what it is you want and placing your complete trust that it's coming into existence in due course.

I do want to take a brief diversion to the topic of detachment. Detachment is one of the main foundations of Buddhism, and when I was younger, I would immerse myself in numerous practices, encouraged by my father. Detachment was something that would serve me more than I could ever know years later and was a concept that would never leave me—detachment from the neediness, wanting something, or holding onto too many things. There is a huge difference between needing something and understanding it is already yours. The two feelings are composed of completely parallel energies. I go into detachment more later in the book, but my point here is that you don't want to feel desperate for the things you want to attract into your life. If you present the energy of lack and neediness to the Universe, that's precisely what you'll end up manifesting. You want to present the energy of already having everything you could ever need. You don't need to fight for anything if you already have it! Like online shopping, you place your order to the Universe, and you get on with your day.

In this instance, the vision board is placing your order. Position it somewhere you can constantly see it. That way, your subconscious mind will be attracting those goals passively—manifesting without lifting a finger!

Another way to widen your vision is using what I call expanders. Expanders are people who will assist you in broadening your vision. Surround yourself with people you can learn from, people who will encourage your growth. When I wanted to attract abundance and wealth, I'd go out of my way to find people online or even within my circle who were already successful female entrepreneurs. I thought, "She comes from a similar background and has been through similar things. If I can relate, surely I can then go out and be like her, right?" If you can choose a person whose experiences you can relate to, this will only instill more belief in your own capabilities to match or even exceed their achievements. Choose people who light up the room—the bestselling authors, the best at whatever they're doing. Find inspiration and encouragement in them.

You can also apply expanders to your love life, choosing to surround yourself with couples who are already in a relationship you wish to emulate. Find power couples who embody what you'd like to have. Start to study and mirror those kinds of behaviors. As always, the only way to look is from a place of love and compassion; removing ego, pride, and jealousy from your world will literally transform your entire life.

Whatever it is you want to attract, use the five people around you to do so. If you haven't met them in person, no problem. The online space holds a magnitude of limitless power and energy. I'd never met any of the five couples I was tuning into face to face when I manifested my husband into my life. I looked at couples like Obama and Michelle or Justin and Hailey. I used to find inspiration in an array of different people, appreciating the beautiful relationships they had. I felt that love as I looked at videos of them and how they were spending their time, and it brought me so much joy.

When you daydream, you actually put yourself into a hypnotic state. It's a trance-like state where your brain begins to perceive life in slow motion, and you just stare. When you're staring, if you learn to take control of it, that can be a powerful state of mind to have at your fingertips. If you can learn to replace any thought with its ideal counterpart—something that you want to attract—start to daydream about that idea, stare as if you're fixated on what's already yours, you're starting to play with your subconscious mind and, consequently, rewire your brain.

With this in mind, be conscious of what you consume visually on TV or in the media. When you watch TV, your conscious mind deactivates, making room for your subconscious mind to come forward, again evoking that trance-like state of fixation. Strict boundaries around what you allow your subconscious mind to consume are essential, especially before you sleep (Remember, that's a prime time when your brain is most receptive).

Seeds plant into the mind like an egg plants into a womb. Be careful of the seeds you sow on your nightly visit to dreamland. If you're consuming endless content around healthy, fun, fulfilling relationships, and that's what you want to attract into your life, brilliant! If, on the other hand, you're allowing the media to negatively invade your headspace, you've got some homework to do.

One of the common struggles when it comes to the Law of Attraction, and the main reason people might not see the results they want, is that they think positively, but they are missing out on translating that into feeling and emotion and then using that feeling as fuel to take action. Are your actions aligning in this way? That's the pillar we're coming to next—taking action.

Remembering to act as if your manifestation is already yours is the most important part of the puzzle! Anything that you want to attract in your life, you can have, but you've got to feel that it's yours. You've got to believe it. Your brain doesn't really know if it's happened yet. Remember to imagine the colors, the smells, the tastes like we do in the MBS method. Repetition is a big part of visualization. If you continuously repeat that same vision in your mind over and over and over, you'll be surprised how quickly its physical manifestation shows up in your life. Repeatedly do things that make you feel empowered, that raise your vibration before moving into the next pillar: taking action.

Pillar Five: Take Inspired Action

This is the final pillar to manifest your desires and create your reality on your terms. This is probably one of the most important pillars because without action, all those thoughts, beliefs, and positive affirmations remain reserved for the reservoir of your imagination. You don't want to fall at the final hurdle. As powerful as the first four pillars are, without completing the final step, you'll go nowhere. You must take action if you're to reach the finish line. All you've ever wanted is right there, so what are you waiting for?

The first tip is to take the goal you established in pillar one, write it down, and get clear on your vision. Before you go to bed every night, write down three smaller goals that work toward your main goal, ones that you're capable of achieving the very next day. Three goals every single day is 1,095 goals a year. Remember, you're becoming an achiever. Do you see how powerful that is?

Let's say, for example, that your goal is to write a book this year. Your three smaller goals for the day could look like finding a publisher, emailing fifty potential publishers, and contacting friends who can add quotes and testimonials to the book. These are three things that are achievable and immediately actionable, giving you a deep sense of satisfaction and accomplishment every single day. When you start to achieve, your energy becomes infectious. Attracting bigger goals takes less effort because you *are* an achiever; it's what you do every day.

While we are on the power of three, I want to point out that the most influential people in history, as with many great minds (e.g., Einstein, Da Vinci, Ludovico), all had one thing in common: they honed their craft. They'd focus intently on their gifts every single day for hours and hours. They removed themselves from the world, often traveling to secluded places to sit, to focus on what they did best—learning, studying, reading, writing, practicing free from any kind of distraction. It was *that* important. For three hours a day, I apply this. I read, write, and learn. It might be listening to a podcast, reading a book, or writing a new chapter of my book. Whatever it may be, I do three hours a day. That's over 1,095 hours a year of practice on my craft! Repetition is the mother of skill, and the only road to mastery is practice.

When I read a book, I try to get into the headspace of that author, as if I'm being personally mentored by them for those three hours I'm reading. Reading from this perspective makes you feel like you're learning it firsthand, actually living the mindset of that person, understanding their thought process, putting yourself in their shoes. Reading is an enormously powerful tool for growth. When we give ourselves the space to learn, we have something valuable to share with others.

There's a famous quote I love: "When the student is ready, the teacher will appear." Having this book in your hands proves your readiness to learn. Whether you allow me to be your mentor and continually guide you on a journey toward your highest level of success or you find another mentor, make sure you really invest in yourself, hone your craft, enroll yourself in that program, improve your mindset, because 80 percent of success is in the mindset while 20 percent is in the action. Mindset is huge, but it's nothing without action. So, take those steps toward your dream every day.

Setting your goal is a brilliant first step, but only if you're prepared to take actionable steps toward it. Here's an exercise I'd like you to try right now. I want you to draw a pyramid with the biggest space at the bottom. In this bottom space, you'll write your urgent tasks, the immediate same-day things you need to happen that day. The middle section of the pyramid is for your goal and the top level is for your ideas. So now you should have your base level, middle level, and your top level filled out.

The part you'll spend the least amount of your time on is your ideas, hence why we put that at the top. Never disregard them though; this is where the magic will eventually happen. Thoughts, where ideas span from, become things, and though small now, these ideas will soon transcend into bigger visions, creating an app or starting a company for example, something you know ties into your large-scale, ultimate goal.

Then we have the middle section, where you've written the goals you want to achieve—writing that book, starting that business. Just getting it down on the page will ignite that spark of motivation and help direct your focus. It's from this section you will choose things that you're going to take action on each day. The urgent tasks lie at the bottom of the pyramid. Examples could include any amalgamation of tasks that need to be done that day—admin, bills, work that (for now) pays the bills, housework, etc. This is what you'd essentially recognize as your immediate to-do list.

Ultimately, you want to get the urgent tasks, the biggest section, out of the way as quickly as possible. Once complete, you can get clear on your goals for the week, the month, or even the year! You'll be breaking down those goals with your three hours of dedication to your craft. And finally, you can branch out to the ideas and strategize ways to implement them. Then it comes back to the morning and evening rituals we spoke about earlier. You might be thinking, "This sounds like a lot of work!" I assure you that when you shift your mindset, opportunities are suddenly everywhere. They are opportunities that have always been there; it's just that with your new perspective, you can see them clearly.

When you have a clear goal that you want to manifest, asking the Universe every day to reveal the signs that let you know you're on the right track can be such a comfort. These could appear as events, people, and places, giving you a glimpse of what to do to serve humanity better.

Bumps in the road are, of course, a part of life, and I'm not here to try and convince you it's always going to be smooth sailing. Chances are, you're going to face some challenges along the way. When you're not having a great day and you're feeling down, you'll notice the lack of appearance of anything that makes you feel good. Why? Because like attracts like! What you put out you will receive! Try shifting that blue mood by giving gratitude, even when you're in your lowest state, like I was when I was unwell. In that state, I'd find gratitude for all the other parts of my body that were functioning. In the same way, when I was broke, I'd give gratitude for all the things I *did* have, like my son. I had gratitude for the fact that my parents had allowed me to come back home so that I wasn't homeless anymore. Shifting those feelings of hopelessness into plentiful feelings of gratitude resulted in me naturally attracting more positivity into my life.

Let's put this into practice right now. Write down five things you are grateful for. Take a moment to do this simple gratitude exercise.

When you've written down your five, write out another column titled: "I am so excited for . . ." and write down five things that you are excited for in your life right now. It could sound something like "I'm so excited to travel to five new countries this year," for example. It could even be something that you haven't planned but you are excited for as though it's happening to you. It can be concretely planned into your future already or an exciting experience you'd like to bring into it! What are you excited for? Write those things down.

Finally, write down five things you're grateful for right now as though they're already yours. Having gratitude for those desirable things that are yet to happen are how you manifest them into your reality! This is exactly how I manifested money back into my life. I was in fifty thousand dollars of debt—fifty thousand! I wrote, "I am so grateful for the $55,000 coming back into my account right now. I am so grateful for this unexpected check I just received in the mail.

I am so excited to own my ability to get out of debt and be free of any financial ties pulling me down." Write it all down. And be specific.

Just three months after I started doing that, I was debt free. I think I made $56,259 to be precise, which was about one thousand dollars more than the amount I was in debt. That really blew my mind! That day, I proved to myself my ability to transform my reality simply by tapping into my mindset. You really do create your own story.

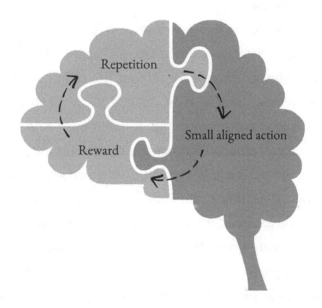

Do this practice every day for twenty-one days. It takes twenty-one days to form a small habit and sixty-six days to form a bigger one. And every day you show up to check that off your list, your brain gets a little spike of dopamine, a neurotransmitter in the reward center of your brain that acts as your personal cheerleader, reminding you that *you are* the achiever you were always born to be.

Take a look at the diagram above of the cognitive loop that happens every time you perform your small, aligned action. You show up for yourself, feel the amazing benefits, and become more and more motivated to keep doing it every time you show up.

Keeping track is a great way to keep yourself accountable. Try filling out the habit tracker on the next page starting today for twenty-one days. Think of these days as twenty-one chances to take another step toward your potential. Why not send this to a friend and commit to holding each other accountable?

So, there you have it. Take action on goals that inspire you to accept your life's mission, and watch it come to fruition before your very eyes. Trust me, when you put work into redefining your mindset, and you believe in your limitless capabilities, you can make anything happen, no matter how dark it may seem at the starting line. You are a manifestation of your own creation.

My daily habit DAY:

	1	2	3	4	5	6	7	8	9	10	11	12	13	14	15	16	17	18	19	20	21

Chapter 7:

From the Moment
to the Outcome

What happens in the space between setting your vision, refining your goals, and actualizing the outcome? One word, honey: hustle. If you really want to achieve everything you desire, you must be willing to do the work. Olympic gold medalist, Michael Phelps, says, "If you want to be the best, you have to do things that other people aren't willing to do." You must exceed any expectation of average. This could translate as waking up earlier in the mornings, daily strategizing toward your dreams, holding sacred space for yourself, giving to others, or excelling physically. Whatever that looks like for you, strongly committing to yourself and your goals by developing that willingness to hustle is fundamental for you to ascend to greatness in any area of your life.

As we alluded to earlier, repeatedly executing aligned actions every day *will* lead you toward success and abundance. And on those days when you don't feel your best, when things don't play out as planned, when you find yourself in an utterly demotivating situation, this is where your ability to dig deep really counts. The more challenges you overcome, and the stronger the resilience you develop, the more you'll cultivate an unshakeable power that will help you push through anything. When you fall down, you'll get back up, because achieving your goals depends on your continuous, long-term persistence.

We've all made the mistake of setting some seemingly inspiring resolutions on January 1 feeling full of motivation, planning illustriously exciting ventures like going to the gym or ditching alcohol or junk food, so why do these always end up fading after only a week or so? Why, time and time again, do people pay a full year's subscription for a gym and only attend during the first month? Because they're aiming for the wrong target! They are depending entirely on motivation with no real purpose behind their goal. This is why what you wish to manifest must be accompanied by a strong, powerful *why* to supply the driving force to keep going until you've done it.

There's a Japanese proverb that says, "Vision without action is a daydream. Action without vision is a nightmare." Do you see how just setting random goals or visions and not aligning your actions will only take you on the road to nowhere?

> *Doing actions with no purpose behind them*
> *drains any energy sources you have and leads*
> *to a life of frustration, anguish, and terror.*

So many people fall short when it comes to taking action, usually because they're afraid of failing (I dive deep into the power of failure in a later chapter). It's that niggling *what if?* That fills them with dread, restricting their movement and growth to the small circle of their comfort zone. But playing safe never allows for growth. In order to evolve, we have to step out of our comfort zones, expose ourselves to new and challenging experiences, push our boundaries, and expand our barriers. Fear is actually one of the lowest vibrational frequencies humans possess, so low it can paralyze us into hostility. Never ever allow fear to take the wheel in life.

It may not feel pleasant at the time, but I strongly believe that every negative situation, every failure, comes with a blessing, often in the form of a powerful lesson. When a scenario arises that you perceive as negative, shift that fear into faith and think, "Who am I not to trust the path the Universe has laid out for me?" Embrace that fear, focus on the outcome you're striving toward; leap and the net will appear! I've felt fear so many times throughout my journey, and if I'd let it make my decisions for me, you wouldn't be reading this book today.

No one, not even successful people, live without fear. The only difference between them and the rest of the world is that they are people who felt the fear and *still* took action. They

harnessed their fears to become the accelerators of their evolution by showing up every freaking day ready to stand up and
look fear in the face.

If you feel stuck in your head right now, this is the perfect time to learn new skills and bring more hustle to every
area of your life—health, relationships, mindset, love, skill
sets, work—and take actions aligned with your bigger goal
every day, no matter how small. Don't waste your time dream-
ing about what you *could* achieve and start achieving. All we
have is this moment right now and look how you're spending
it! Here in this very moment, you're reading these words and
learning about the Law of Attraction. The past doesn't exist,
nor does the future. All that exists is right now.

It's worth noting that there's always an opposite extreme
to avoid as well. There is a fine balance between striving so
much you wind up burned out, overworked, and heading ten
steps back from where you came from and striving for more
while acknowledging where you're at. With constant conscious awareness as your guiding light, you get better at learning what you need and when—when it's time to turn up the
heat and when it's time to cool off and take a break.

Everything building up to this point aims to give you the
tool kit to literally *Be It Until You Become It*—to be who you
were always born to be—but this is a good point to remind you
that being it to become it really does go both ways.

I had a client a few years ago, let's call him Dan for his
discretion. Now first off, Dan is such a good guy, yet he was

in a downward spiral, drowning himself in drink with multiple sexual partners. He seemed completely lost. He had no direction, no purpose, and too much money for his own good. I had a chat with him one day and just asked him outright, "Is this really who you want to be?"

I don't think he could quite believe the words coming out of my mouth at first, so I continued to spell it out. Sometimes all you need to wake up is someone on the outside looking in to voice what everyone else is thinking. I told him, "The world sees you as the joker at the party, as the womanizer, the playboy. Do you like those titles? Because every time you repeat those behaviors, you're becoming more of a fool. Is that really who you are?" I told him to give me a ring if he was ready to let that person go.

I know these words sound cutthroat and cruel, but unless I held that mirror right up to his face, he'd never have heard me. About six months later, my phone rang. It was Dan. "Alright, you've done it for thousands of others, maybe there's a chance this transformation could work for me. I'll do it." He later told me he was taking medication for depression and had been through numerous therapists without a spec of improvement. I put Dan through everything I've shared with you in this book, as well as mentoring him one on one and putting him through a few of my coaching programs. And to his amazement, little by little, day by day, Dan learned that he was worthy of love, that he didn't need alcohol to numb his pain anymore. He gave up drinking completely, realizing he could use that wealth of time and resources for something better.

The crazy thing with Dan was that he was a very wealthy man already, so wealthy that it became another source of addiction, making money just for the sake of making money with no real purpose behind it other than as a tool to numb his pain. Following my mentorship, Dan developed his business in a more purposeful way and even started a charity. He learned he had a plethora of transferable skills he could use to do an immense amount of good in the world. And with every ounce, Dan started to feel whole again. He became his purpose instead of becoming his addiction.

Whatever you do, always be grateful and present. Focus only on what's in your control—your routines, your morning and evening rituals, your vision. Focus on that, and you can create the reality of your choosing.

Chapter 8:

Harness Your Unlimited Power

I n his book *The Power of Your Subconscious Mind*, Joseph
Murphy says, "As you sow in your subconscious mind, so
shall you reap in your body and environment."[21] What seeds
are you planting in your subconscious mind? Are they seeds of
sadness and anger? Or are you planting seeds of joy, love, and
compassion? Because whatever it is that you're planting, so
shall you reap and receive.

To become the best at sowing seeds you can, I'm going
to teach you four basic tools to tune into an ultimate state of
self-awareness. Only with conscious awareness can we harness the power of our thoughts and the unlimited power within.

The first tool is disconnecting—disconnecting from all
your devices and from any distractions. Be brave enough to
be alone with your own thoughts. You must do this every day.
How many minutes a day do you take to meditate? How much
time do you invest in just sitting and being in your own pres-

ence, in your own energy? Answering these questions can feel confronting, but it will give you insight into where you're starting from so that you can plan your route ahead.

The second tool is to visualize actively letting go. Bring to your mind anything holding you back and imagine every limiting belief, every self-sabotaging thought and feeling, dripping off your body like running water dripping onto the floor. Let go of everything that's not the ideal version of you. You might want to write down all those past behaviors coming to the surface, making a commitment to not repeat them again by drawing a big line through the middle of them, crossing them out. As you do this, repeat the words: "I don't need to do this anymore."

The third tool is creating an expanse of space in your mind to bring in the childlike curiosity we talked about with the five pillars. I want you to focus on finding space between your thoughts here to widen that space. This might take some practice but keep at it. We must make space to allow ourselves to ponder questions like: What energizes you? Where is your focus and where do you want it to be? One question that gives you instant insights on where your focus lies is: What do you spend your money on? Most people don't realize that where they spend their money is where their attention is going. As Tony Robbins says, "Where focus goes, energy flows." Are you investing the resources you have in yourself, in things that help you grow and become a better person? Or are your funds leaking into self-sabotaging behaviors that feed on your insecurities? You'll always find that the aspects you don't want to give attention to are the ones you're procrastinating on. Write down the answers to these questions in your journal and try not to take it too seriously. Judgment is not invited to the party. Be curious and playful here. Write down what comes up for you.

Tool number four is about introducing yourself to you as that high-flying god or goddess. Cast yourself in your favorite role in a movie produced by *your conscious awareness* titled *Living My Best Life*. How does that person act? What are they wearing? What are they doing that day? What does their day look like? Step into that role with all your senses and really feel it; embody it. I do this quite often, because I truly enjoy seeing the results it brings to my life. I feel so swept up in the moment, fully awakened and alive. I can even hear the noises around me in my visualization. It's a really phenomenal experience.

A lot of athletes actually use this visualization technique before they compete, mentally rehearsing the race, using all their senses so their mind stores it as a memory. When they experience it in reality, their brain is convinced they've already won gold a few million times. There's zero doubt in their ability to perform to their highest potential. You can do this with anything you want to manifest. Get clear on what you want to achieve and create the experience first in your mind using these four basic steps of disconnecting, letting go, getting curious, and embodying that experience. You've got to align the behavior to become it.

If you apply any one of these tools—or better still, apply all of them—you'll soon begin experiencing the shifts as you start to tap into that unlimited conscious awareness, also known as your abundant supply of transformational energy.

In *The Science of Getting Rich,* Wallace D Wattles describes this energy in the most incredible way. He reminds us that energy is everywhere. There is this substance that you can't see, and its primary function is to immediately transfer its energy into any thought, using the thought like we use public transport, jumping onto any train your mind wanders to. So, as soon as you think of something, boom! It's imprinted into this invisible energy field around you.

> *"Quantum Science suggests the existence of many possible futures for each moment of our lives. Each future lies in a state of rest until it is awakened by choices made in the present" —Gregg Bradden.*

Take Gregg's proposition into consideration when you're choosing the thoughts you're allowing into your mind. This idea is nothing new, by the way. This is ancient wisdom that's been around for thousands upon thousands of years. And what I'm sharing with you here is how you really can transform your life with these ancient secrets passed down from our ancestors and a bit of modern science.

Decide which emotions no longer belong to you. You are now in the role of your future self. If you want to be abundant and wealthy, you no longer have space to accept draining thoughts of scarcity and lack. If you want to be healthy, you cannot allow any diminishing thoughts into your mind. Fearful thoughts can be acknowledged but not accepted as truth. You have to rewire this new version of you from the inside out. So, take the time to do these practices. They have the potential to change your life forever.

Chapter 9:

Self-Belief + Self-Love = Magic

Most of us grew up in a society where we were expected to meet certain physical, mental, emotional, and economic standards. Social media, something that's become a regular part of so many people's lives, is guilty of mistakenly teaching us that we should be perfect, that we should be living an airbrushed life. Unfortunately, this has put most of us in a constant state of frustration and self-hatred for not being able to meet those ideological, disproportionally warped standards, when in reality, the unique beauty within each of us is where we should be focusing. How awful would the world be if we all looked the same, had the same lives, and did all the same things, like some kind of designer Groundhog Day? I must admit, on social media, I wasn't always as transparent as I am now. I used to promote a twenty-four hour, wonderful, happy lifestyle too. And you would have believed it! You would have assumed I was in the most happy, harmonious family and relationship, when in reality, I felt like I was drowning in silence—and nobody knew it. Things are not always as they first appear, and any standards you derive from pictures on social media are completely false. Philosopher Ralph Waldo Emerson summed it up well when he said, "To be yourself in a world that is constantly trying to make you something else is the greatest accomplishment."

When you quit trying to fit in, you unlock the strength to reach your full capacities—which are yours alone—through the two most powerful forces on the planet: self-love and self-belief. Loving yourself comes with accepting everything that makes you who you are, all those quirks and gorgeous little details in the fabric that makes you. It's putting your well-being first and having the courage to say "no" when something doesn't resonate. It's forgiving any wrongs and recognizing that it's okay to make mistakes. It is giving thanks for everything you are and everything that's made you. Appreciating yourself in this way massively aids your physical, psychological, and spiritual growth. It promotes empathy, authenticity, healthy relationships, confidence, and your overall ability to achieve. It's very important to identify any vicious cycles of self-loathing, negative self-talk, bad habits, or self-neglect and break them—before they break you. Nurture your relationship with yourself, because at the end of the day, the only person you'll ever have is yourself.

Your deepest inner self-beliefs and thoughts become your outer reality and the life you are experiencing.

Words hold the power to define our relationships, our performance, and our well-being. As writer Brendan McCaughey warns, "Don't ignore the power of words. This power will play a perpetual role in your life. Our ability to find love and joy rely entirely on the frequency of those words being sought, expressed, received, and understood. The emotions we feel, the events we experience, and our ability to interact with other humans are all controlled by language. If we want more control, and more agency in our lives we can start with a greater understanding of the potential power in what we say to ourselves and others."[22] Your inner dialogue can either be your best support or your worst enemy.

I like to think of it this way: imagine you are holding the most precious little baby in your arms. You can be thinking about your own child (I always do). This baby is filled with light and love, and its only interest is to be happy and give you love in return. He or she looks at you with innocence, authenticity, and emotional vulnerability. Now imagine saying horrible, aggressive, hateful, diminishing things to this baby. Could you even do it? Would you do it? Most likely your answer is "no." So, what makes you think you are any less than that precious baby you are holding in your arms? *You too* deserve to be treated with love, respect, patience, and acceptance. Be mindful of the way you speak to yourself. Notice the tone of your inner dialogue. And every time you find yourself speaking out of tongue, remember the baby. If you wouldn't say those things to the baby, you shouldn't be saying them to yourself.

Something that I incorporate on a daily basis that helps me cultivate my self-love and confidence is affirmations. Affirmations are my secret weapon and one of my favorite tools for aligning my mindset with the direction of my goals and dreams. An affirmation is a simple but powerful statement that helps strengthen the connection between your subconscious and your conscious mind. The more we strengthen this connection, the more resilient we become when facing difficult or challenging circumstances. Whatever you *affirm* to yourself, be that positive or negative, your mind believes and accepts, so it becomes your personal truth. As Henry Ford so plainly puts it: "Whether you think you can or think you can't, you are right."

Every morning, I look at myself in the mirror and I say, "I am the powerful creator of my life, I am confident, I am enough, I am healthy, I am wealthy, I am abundant, I am free, I am safe, I am loved, and I am blessed." Sometimes I just say it in my head while in the shower or doing housework. This is a game changer when it comes to shifting the way you see and treat yourself, and therefore, your whole outlook on life.

Self-love and self-belief are what allow you to work hard for your dreams despite anyone else's opinion of you or your dreams. They define your reality. Remember, whatever you are manifesting into your life is a reflection of your feelings of self-worth. You deserve to be happy, you deserve to have all those things you want, you deserve to be loved, and you deserve abundance. Truly believe that you are worthy of all those things. No one else is going to give you the confidence to create your own reality! Believe, deep down from the bottom of your heart, that you can achieve anything and everything you desire. You are capable of absolutely anything, so start acting like it. Treat yourself like you would like everyone else to treat you.

Loving yourself and giving yourself the strength and the confidence to go about your dreams is something no one can take away from you. You'll create magic in your life. Inner peace also allows you to provide greater value to others. Our thoughts, words, and actions are a direct result of our inner dialogue. If what you hold inside is love, gratitude, and appreciation, that's what you'll be transmitting to others. You'll cultivate healthy relationships, attract a bigger community to your business, and create abundance everywhere you go.

I started my career mostly through Instagram. I understood from the get-go the power of sharing my value with others and trusted that bigger and better opportunities were on the way, so I bought an Instagram account. I knew that this was the shortcut to really getting onto other world leaders' radars and going straight to the top. I bought it from someone who had a similar audience as mine, so adding my content to her page was an easy transition. It was those initial numbers combined with my valuable content at the time that helped me get the attention that acted as the catapult for my career.

Remember when I talked about knocking on digital doors? When I first started, I'd send direct messages to at least fifty people a day. That equated to 18,250 new people *per year*.

Right from the beginning, I knew that I wanted to be on stage with the greatest names out there: Tony Robbins, Jesse Itzler, Daymond John, Gary Vee, Dan Fleyshman, and Andy Frisella, to name a few. I wanted to get on that frequency, learn from them, share knowledge with them, and connect with them on a deeply conscious level. I knew if I wanted to gain respect from those kinds of beings, I had to be unknockably confident in my own skin with a steadfast belief in the value I had to offer. I had to know my worth. So, when I knocked on their door, I said: "This is who I am. And here's what I can do for you." I'd leave a personalized voice message for every single one of these incredible people telling them why I wanted to connect with them and how my work could benefit them. I needed just one "yes" to start the ignition.

David Meltzer answered the call first. He agreed to come on my show, which at the time was just a video call that I would share online, but once David granted me the key to my ignition, everyone else started saying "yes" too. I knew this level of content would give me visibility and give their audience value. If it wasn't for my belief in the value I was offering, none of this would've been possible.

My next "yes" was from Jim Kwik, the number-one mind coach in the world. David started the ignition, but Jim allowed me to take my foot off the clutch completely. I was in foot-to-floor acceleration. The rest is history.

Since then, I've gone on to work with people I greatly admire and largely owe my success to, people like Lisa Nichols,

John Assaraf, Dr. Demartini, and many, many more. The value I was offering, combined with the wisdom all these people had to share, gave rise to my podcast, which is now rated as one of the top ten podcasts in the world alongside the likes of Joe Rogan, Tim Ferriss, Jay Shetty, and more. I feel honored to be able to stand on the podium with them. And it all started with me knowing my worth, knowing I had value to share with the world, and taking action through my social platforms.

Know your worth, believe in your power, give yourself the love you deserve, and see your life change in ways you could previously only dream of. When you're filled with love and abundance, you operate on that vibration and radiate an intoxicating energy of light. Focus on giving value, love, and light to yourself, so you can share and spread that value with the rest of the world.

Chapter 10:

The Three Most Important Laws of Manifesting

The Law of Oneness and Potentiality

The Law of Oneness and Potentiality states that *under-lying the infinite diversity of life is the unity of one all-pervasive spirit. There is no separation.* Once you understand that everything is energy, be it visible or not, you'll start to see how everything is interconnected and how much influence you have on the world around you. That Universal higher realm is where all aspects of your consciousness manifest. When your creative power aligns with the Universal creative power, you'll be able to create a reality beyond your wildest dreams.

Isolation is merely a figment of our imagination. In truth, we are connected to every single person and thing in the universe because everything is made up of the same stuff: stardust.

With this in mind, we can take the golden rule of "don't do to others what you don't want to be done to you" to a whole other level. Any time you talk behind someone's back, judge another person, or put negative vibes onto someone or something else in any way, shape, or form, the collateral damage comes back your way and blackens your surrounding environment.

It really is a free for all when it comes to the limitless creativity and creation the Universe beholds, because *you are* the Universe, *you ar*e that energy, and that limitless field of possibilities is *already* within you.

The Law of Detachment

The Law of Detachment states that *you must let go of your desired outcome in order for it to manifest.* Attachment is fear—fear of not being able to reach that desired outcome. Incessant thoughts of when and how you can possibly reach it deter your mind from ever taking action, building a stone wall of insecurity around your own creative power.

Attachment can also manifest as trying to control something or someone to feel secure. Ironically, the outcome is usually the complete opposite of security in the form of spiraling depression, stress, and obsessive compulsive behaviors. Instead, when you've freed your mind from needing to control your outcome, you unleash an unquestionable belief in yourself. This is a superpower that supplies your mind with infinite knowledge of your creative powers to achieve that outcome and many more to follow.

Detachment is the symbol of abundance. American author William Powers puts it beautifully when he says, "Your life will be in flow, if you let go. Everything that is meant to follow you will do so."[23]

The Law of Reciprocity

The Law of Reciprocity is a basic law of social psychology. It affirms that *whatever you give out to others will be reciprocated.* It is a basic but powerful norm that weaves into the tapestry of our humanity. The workings of the Universe are a continuous exchange, a sea of harmonious interactions that happen between all things. We give and we receive. But it always starts with giving as far as attracting abundance is concerned.

You see, when you give with the pure intention of serving the world, people feel indebted to you after receiving such positive things with no expectation of any reciprocation. They'll want to give something to you in return, usually in greater proportions, so your actions will always be reciprocated when you come from a place of service.

I like to constantly remind myself, "If you're not giving, you're not living." Serve the world around you. Light someone else's candle every single day and create a powerful wave of positive deeds and gestures. Trust me, you will be reciprocated. I call this my Candle Effect. Do a kind deed or goodwill gesture for someone today and that someone will go on and light somebody else's candle and then that someone will go on and light somebody else's candle and very quickly you have lit up the whole world just from one smile you made to a stranger in the street. You can also blow someone's candle out by spreading your bad mood or saying something unkind to someone and then that someone will go on and blow out somebody else's candle and so on and so forth. So you can see how you can delight the world just as quickly as you can light it up. So will you choose to like someone's candle today or blow it out?

Chapter 11:

Transform Negative Energy into Positive Energy

We all have challenging days when we face difficult situations that crumble any sense of positivity we may have woken up with. Knowing how to manage these situations and shift those negative energies into positive energies is paramount. As I've said more times than I care to count, I have firsthand experience finding the blessings and teachings behind adversity. So, before succumbing to that victim mentality, when something negative occurs, look for the hidden teaching behind it. It might be hard to see at first, like a lone streetlamp in the thickest fog, but know this: the Universe will never give you something you can't handle.

Shifting your negatives into positives isn't a matter of ignoring the adversities you're facing. It's finding acceptance for what is that takes you from grieving to healing. It's giving your energy, even if there's only an ounce of it left, to faith and possibility over fear. It's understanding that ultimately something is happening *for* you, not *to* you. Though not easy to hear at the time, there's always growth hidden between the cracks in the walls of adversity. Sometimes you might feel those walls caving in until you feel like you're no longer able to cope, but dare to look for the cracks, and you'll always see the light shining through from the other side.

One of the things adversity gives us is tools to manage situations in the future, helping us know ourselves better and preparing us for what is yet to come. If everything was always sunshine and daisies, there would be no sense of achievement, because there's no purpose in working hard when there's nothing to overcome. We'd take everything for granted. Adversity is a necessary part of life, and how you perceive it can be the difference between an earthquake and a volcano. Don't wait under a table for your whole world to come crashing down. Be the volcano and ignite the lava within you.

I remember learning about an experiment in which scientists grew trees indoors so that they wouldn't be affected by any exterior factors—no wind, no rain, no fresh air. What ended up happening was mind-blowing; the trees only grew to a fraction of their usual proportions. The wind was responsible for the tree's growth, making the bark and the roots dig deep into the earth and create a strong foundation.

Just as trees need wind, humans need to struggle. The adversity in our lives allows us to grow and build the deep-rooted resilience necessary to thrive. Without those storms, we'd stay stagnant. Appreciate the tough moments and the struggles yet to come. Be patient and know they will always serve a higher purpose in your life.

Whenever you find yourself knee-deep in those negative situations, try writing down a new positive affirmation about yourself and the moment you're going through. Stick it around your house and look at that affirmation multiple times per day. As I mention earlier in the book, absorbing affirmations, even in passing, embeds the belief into your subconscious and shifts your vibration to a higher frequency. You might write something along the lines of: "This situation does not define me, I trust the Universe has my back, and I know this will serve my higher purpose. I have the power within me to overcome this. I will turn this mess into my message. I am safe, and I choose to let go and trust." Write it down on a post-it note and stick it somewhere visible. It's not even something you need to practice or read out loud. The more you pass it, the deeper the message is embedded into your subconscious mind.

Another really helpful thing to do is moving your body and literally shaking it off. Try it. Stand up right now and just shake your body—flail your arms, tap your feet, dance around. No one's watching. Shake off all that negative energy, that fear or frustration. Jump up and down. Do whatever feels good for you! Physically moving your body is the fastest route to a clearer head and an even sharper mind. Shaking swaps all that cortisol in your body, the primary stress hormone, for those feel-good endorphins, another neurotransmitter that acts to increase feelings of pleasure and well-being and reduce feelings of pain and discomfort. Rebuild your chi, the vital force within you, and allow the energy to soar through your body like a wave.

Round out any form of exercise by lying down, hands by your sides with palms facing up, holding all your focus on the palms of your hands. Inhale courage and exhale fear with an audible sigh of relief. Do you feel it? That tingle in your palms, your feet, your arms, and your heart is your vital force. That's your chi. Once you feel that energy in your palms, place one hand over your abdomen and one hand over your heart. Transmit the energy into your body; feel the chi warming and renewing every cell. Finish by whispering "I've got this" to yourself—because you do.

Chapter 12:

Transformative Failure

F ailure—even hearing that tightens most people's stomach into knots, casting them back to the humiliation they felt the last time they fell flat on their face. But failure is so important for us to grow and learn!

Many assume that failing means it's all over, but what if we flipped that and saw it as the beginning, taking failure as nothing other than feedback? It doesn't mean you aren't good enough, smart enough, or strong enough; it's actually completely unrelated to any of your talents and abilities. If you've failed, it means you tried, and that is already a successful outcome. Every time you fall down, you get back up a little stronger. Start seeing every setback as a setup for your next win. Every failure is just the Universe's way of serving you another opportunity to try again, to try a different technique and learn about you and/or your business in new and exciting ways.

It's all about your mindset and how you perceive the situation. The problem is never the problem. The way you think about the problem is the problem. Read that again.

Having feelings of shame, distress, worry, or worthlessness is normal when something crashes and burns. But it's up to you to shift that low vibration quickly and adjust your approach with your new understanding that failure always brings new opportunities and even better outcomes in the long run. Get used to failing, because truthfully, for every "yes" you get, there will be ninety-nine times you get "no" before it. You just don't hear about the instances of "no" as much in other people's success stories.

According to Professor Christopher Myers from the University of Michigan, "The recognition of failure as a learning opportunity encourages people to take a more resilient, developmental approach to the inevitable failures that happen in life (rather than hiding, avoiding or ignoring them), helping to motivate their learning and improvement."[24] In fact, in an experiment held by Myers, Francesca Gino of Harvard University, and Bradley Staats from the University of North Carolina, they found that "When individuals accept and internalize a failure, they learn and improve their performance significantly more than those who externalize or blame their failure on outside forces."[25] Failure is just another stepping-stone on the way to living your best life.

The screw-ups also make for great stories. When have you heard a success story without at least one mention of failure?

We've all been there, me included. Every time I look back at my failures, I'm humbled by the great teachings they've brought me, and I feel so grateful. The successes are one thing, but I learned so much more from the times things *didn't* turn out the way I'd hoped for. If it weren't for all those rejections or failed attempts, I wouldn't be where I am today. I've said in multiple interviews, "Do not look or judge me for who I am now but for how many times I fell down and got back up, because that's what really made all the difference."

Rejection can smack you down and devastate you for a moment, but it can also lift you up, motivating and empowering you to keep going. When you stay there on the floor, whining and moaning as a victim, you develop a negative outlook on the world. The funny part is that the rest of the world will move on. Opportunities will literally step over you, and you'll still be there, hung up over something that could have pushed you further if you'd only gotten up off of the floor.

If you look at anybody at the top, how many times do you think they were knocked down? How many times were they thrown off their high horse and back onto that floor? And how many times did they get back up? That's how you judge someone. That's a measure of success right there. So, ask yourself, how many times do you get back up?

I know at times all you want to do is give up and lie face down for a while. But when that feeling arises, it only means success is just around the corner. It's right there at your fingertips! Half the time, you have no idea how close you really are.

It's like babies learning to walk. When they finally stand and try to walk, they fall down. But do they stop? Do they think that walking is not for them? No way! They find the strength in those teeny legs to get back up and try again. They might cry and struggle a million times over, but they get back up on their feet and fall until they make it. Be like the baby. It's okay to cry, but keep getting back up. Learn how to transform failure and give yourself the gifts of confidence, strength, and power to keep going no matter what.

To build this skill (yes, overcoming failure is a skill you learn like any other), be sure to get out of your comfort zone every day. Explore new things. Try something you are afraid to fail at. Expose yourself to those situations repeatedly. Just as a muscle has to tear a little to get stronger, being the worst in the room at something new will make you more adaptable and brave! As Tony Robbins puts it, "The ability to move out of your comfort zone in regular, positive ways allows you to strike the right balance between certainty and uncertainty. Pushing your boundaries can make you more productive, more adaptable and more creative. As you push your personal boundaries, you train your brain to adapt to new situations and create new neural pathways that make you a better problem-solver, decision-maker and leader. You truly become unstoppable."[26] Get used to the idea that staying in your comfort zone won't take you anywhere.

Another great practice I like to incorporate is actively voicing my failures openly with other people. Here I am now, sharing them with you! Doing this helps shift that feeling of shame into feeling proud of your courage to try. Talk about failure openly and transparently with your family and friends. Ask them what they failed at recently. You'll soon realize that everyone flops in different ways, each one as beautiful as the next. Never be ashamed of your failures; they make you.

Benjamin Franklin said, "If you fail to plan, you plan to fail." I've found this to be true in every area of my life. While failure is a wonderful opportunity for growth, planning ahead is a great way to eliminate unnecessary failures. If you're going to fail, at least make it a great big flop, not a silly mistake like not being organized or punctual. That's just being lazy. So, what's your plan? What is the big picture in your mind? What are the daily steps you're taking toward achieving it?

Evaluating the reason behind each of your failures without judgment will always help you form your next aligned action toward success. Any perceived problem is simply an invitation to break your goal down into a series of smaller tasks. Get excited about your problems; they help highlight anything that's not working and better align you or your business to greater success.

Let's put this into context in a practical sense. When a problem arises, acknowledge those natural feelings that come up, accept them fully, and then switch your focus to finding a solution. Curiously and playfully investigate how this situation fits into your wider plan and begin the process of whittling it down into smaller, manageable chunks. Forget shaming yourself for "doing it wrong" or "not being good enough." No, honey. You sit in that moment and allow it to set you up for the onward journey.

Another tactic I encourage to avoid unnecessary failures is having proper time management. Learn how to manage your time effectively. Create balance between work, relationships, and personal development. Good time management aids productivity, helping you to work smart not hard, by organizing all your tasks and keeping a clear head. Doing daily or weekly to-do lists, schedules (and obviously, committing to them) are great tools to better help you manage your time more efficiently.

One specific method I particularly love is an action grid. You create a grid with four different columns, with the tasks of highest priority written on the far left, your goals in the second column, actionable steps toward your goals in the third, and then time on the right.

Under the first column, write down all the things you need to do that day. Write them in order of urgency, and then sit back and look at them. In the next column, note your goals. What things are you working toward? These can be things like writing a new book, obtaining new sources of passive income, strengthening your physical body, or giving more energy to your relationships. Write it down and be specific. Now, evaluate the first two columns. Which actions from the first column are actually aligned with your desired goals? Sometimes we get caught up doing the urgent things, but not the important things. Learn to tell the difference.

Now for the third column, rewrite your to-do list, prioritizing those things that will progress you toward achieving your goals. What are those tasks? Is it doing some digital door knocking? Is it finally sitting down to write that first chapter? Whatever it is, write it down. These are your actionably aligned steps for the day that I talk about earlier in the book.

Finally, in the fourth column, write down the amount of time you need to devote to each activity you're setting out to achieve for the day. How long do you need to dedicate to achieve the results you want in each task? Does each session align with your deadline and bigger plan? This grid is your new way of starting every week. Prioritize your tasks according to the goals you want to reach and manage your time accordingly.

Acknowledge both your wins and your failures. Both are an important part of the formula for the never-ending journey toward abundance, wealth, and the life of your dreams. Be willing to fail and be willing to learn. Treat your falls with humor, patience, and love, and know that if someone is not failing, they are not even trying.

Chapter 13:

Manifestation Mistakes

S
o far in this book, I focus on different methods and the step-by-step process of achieving what you want. By now, you'll have solidified some fundamental processes for cultivating the right mindset, having a clear vision of what you want, detaching from outcome, taking aligned action, being consistent, taking daily steps toward your main goal, and transforming the negatives into positives.

But we haven't covered what *not* to do when trying to manifest.

After working with hundreds of clients, I have found five areas that are the most common no-goes when it comes to manifestation.

1. Self-sabotaging emotions and traumas remain trapped in your body, so you can't effectively manifest what you want.

This is the biggest mistake I see people make. They spend loads of time working on what they want, but they totally avoid doing the inner work to make space for bringing it in. It's like trying to fill a bucket of dirty water with clean water. It kind of works, but it's a slow and arduous process, it's pretty messy, and you never clear out the bad stuff completely. The most dangerous part of doing this is that you don't know what you don't know. Some unhealed traumas stay unrealized for years. The traumatic event doesn't have to be major, but understanding that something in your story impacted you and needs healing is the only way to filter out all the dirty water in your bucket.

In the age of modern science technology, childhood trauma can now be measured via our brain waves. Brain waves are the electric pathways of communication between brain neurons, and they produce different frequencies and vibrations. Depending on the brain wave's bandwidth, its function varies. According to the London Clinic, *Brainworks*, brain waves are best understood as "a continuous spectrum of consciousness; from slow, loud and functional—to fast, subtle, and complex." They explain that "our brainwaves change according to what we're doing and feeling. When slower, broader brainwaves are dominant we can feel tired, slow, sluggish, or dreamy. The higher, fastest frequencies are dominant when we feel wired, or hyper-alert."[27]

The five most common categories of brain waves are as follows: Delta waves, Theta waves, Alpha waves, Beta waves, and Gamma waves. Each type of brain wave facilitates different states of being, such as sleep, deep meditative states of healing, intuition, learning and focus, etc. Knowing how to access these states and educating yourself about the differing brain waves and their functions gives you the power to consciously change your reality.

Delta waves, one of the slowest, and thought to be the loudest, brain waves, occur during profound meditation and deep sleep. They are connected with the qualities of empathy, healing, regeneration, and antiaging. This is why having good sleeping habits and getting those deep, restorative eight hours of sleep is so important.

Theta waves happen in similar moments as Delta, but they exclude any incoming external information, allowing a deeper sense and a more panoramic perspective of everything within us. Through states of deep meditation and sleep, the Delta state promotes learning, memory processing, intuition and foresight, creativity, dreams, and the deepest relaxation. In the Theta state, we access our subconscious mind, cracking open our fears, traumas, and all that information lodged in the very depths of our subconscious.

The Alpha waves produce more active states of mind, fueling our focus and productivity. They thrust us back into the present moment and drive positive thinking, the flow state, energized relaxation, motor coordination, problem-solving, alertness, learning, engagement with the environment, and tackling stressful tasks.

Beta waves have a much higher frequency than any of the waves mentioned above. These waves are the masters behind our regular, day to day states of consciousness. They're responsible for our ability to perform cognitive tasks, think logically and be attentive, cast judgment, perform mental and physical activities, and experience proprioception (an awareness of where you are in space). Beta waves also have three subcategories:

1. Beta one: Where we absorb all new information and enter an introspective state. Put simply, we look inward.
2. Beta two: Where logical thinking, active problem-solving, high levels of energy, high-level cognitive performance, and engagement occurs.
3. Beta three: Where complex thinking, high levels of excitation, anxiety, stress, and arousal happen.

And finally, the fastest, highest-frequency brain waves are Gamma waves. Attributed to fast and quiet transmission of information initiating states of concentration, love, altruism, positive virtues, perception, cognitive enhancement, expanded consciousness, spiritual awakening, and growth. This state is only accessible by silencing the mind, hence the heavenly gift of meditation.

In a study published by Frontiers in behavioral neuroscience, researchers found that people with the lowest scores on the childhood trauma questionnaire showed significantly increased

Delta, Beta one, Beta two, Beta three, and Gamma brain wave activity, as well as a significantly decreased Alpha power. This translates into the following hypothesis: people with a greater degree of trauma have more trouble accessing deeply meditative states, and thus, achieving high levels of mental and physical activity. They also present more naturally high levels of anxiety, stress, and continuous negative thought patterns.[28] It's no wonder that some of us have so much trouble trying to meditate.

Many try to embark on this great quest of growth and manifestation while completely forgetting about cleansing and releasing those past traumas and long-standing limiting beliefs beforehand. Most people who miss this crucial step are dumbfounded as to *why* they are having trouble attracting abundance and assume the process itself must be the problem. In reality, they're simply suffering with a case of *traumatitis,* a subconscious lingering trauma that's been there so long, the person suffering the condition has come to accept that weight on their shoulders as a part of them, despite it having zero value in terms of their progression. If you keep those things locked inside you, you'll forever struggle to access your higher self, if you manage it at all. The study I mention above proves that it's so crucial for you to avoid making this mistake. Let go and heal to attract bigger and better things.

2. You don't know how to access the different brain states to manifest your desires.

Meditating without a purpose is like trying to dig a hole without a shovel; it's boring, it's muddy, and the results of hours of effort are largely disappointing. It has no *real* impact on your reality. The best secret I learned studying with my meditation master and reading books on ancient cultures is that they used different breathing techniques for different things. Just like science proved Galileo was right about the solar system, it has proved our ancestors right about using these breathing techniques. The breathing techniques used for millennia have now been scientifically proven to help us access altered brain states by shifting our brain waves.

By gaining access to controlling your desired brain wave state, mostly through meditation, you'll unlock the door to consciously create the life you desire. You'll be able to gain the knowledge, notate the practice, and then repeat, repeat, repeat. Become the master of accessing different brain wave states to facilitate reaching your specific goal. Just closing your eyes and *trying to meditate* without a purpose won't take you any further than the floor you're sitting on; however, now that you know the different types of brain waves we have access to and the benefit each one of them instigates, you can pair breathing techniques and meditations with the specific state you wish to access. That's what I did in my MBS method: I paired the right breathing technique with the correct meditation and objective to take control of my own body and mind.

3. You're surrounding yourself with the wrong people.

A lot of us don't acknowledge the effect the people around us have on our energy. You are a direct reflection of the five people you spend the most time with. This includes your boss, your colleagues, your friends, your partner, and your family. These close relationships contribute to all aspects of your being, including your habits, your interests, your aspirations, your beliefs, and even your income. Whatever you want your life to look like, you must surround yourself with energy that emulates that vision to bring yourself into alignment. Your close support group should feel safe, empowering, uplifting, and positive.

Our brain and our neurons work in a very intricate, fascinating way. We all possess mirror neurons, which ultimately help us learn through imitation and gain an understanding of the spectrum of human emotions. They are an essential part of our human brain that contributes greatly to the success of our social relationships, education, and development. From infancy, we learn by copying. Have you ever felt like you needed to yawn after seeing somebody else yawn? Have you ever started giggling impulsively after hearing a titter of laughter over your shoulder? Or perhaps you've felt sad when seeing someone else cry or grieved despite nothing actually being wrong with your immediate circumstances? These are all examples of our mirror neurons at work. The same way our reality reflects our internal mapping, we mirror our outer surroundings and environment. This is why surrounding yourself with the right people is massively important.

In a seminar directed by Dr. Dawson Church, he led a crowd of around two hundred people into a deep state of meditation while, in the back of the room, two neuroscientists measured some of the participants' brain waves through an electroencephalogram (EEG). Some of the participants were experienced meditators while others had never done a single meditation in their lives. The results were shocking. They found that the people who had never had a meditative experience were immediately able to enter a deep meditative state by imitating the other participants in the audience! Through mirroring, they not only were able to learn a new skill but they were also able to elevate their state of consciousness and have a real introspective experience.

If you surround yourself with highly driven, positive, abundant, and powerful manifestors, it is only a matter of time before you *become* one of them. If, on the other hand, your close circle is filled with negative, scarcity-driven, problem-focused minds, that is exactly who you will become.

4. You are not understanding the signs from the Universe and not appreciating the little things in your current reality.

Whether you're consciously aware of it or not, the Universe is in constant communication with you. How often would you say you're completely in the now? Totally and utterly present? Would you notice if the Universe gave you a sign that your manifestation was on the way? Would you hear the call if the Universe sent you a challenge to see how much you *really* want to manifest the things you're putting out?

Many people believe that when they ask for something, the Universe will instantly respond, but that's not always the case. Notice the little things around you right now, and bear in mind that *there are no coincidences.* What do the little things tell you about your current reality and the status of your current manifestations? Appreciate these as communication and learn to take notice of them. Give thanks for your current reality and be open to receiving every single sign from the Universe, as seemingly insignificant as it might be. When you start noticing the signs, you'll be able to understand your journey, providing you with the tools to take clearer and faster actions toward your desires.

5. You aren't focusing enough on feeling good.

Remember, you attract what you are embodying, so *feeling good* is essential to attract more great experiences into your life. Sometimes people get caught up in the routines and rituals and they end up mindlessly sleepwalking through their intended actions in the hopes that they will manifest what they want the most. But that emotional connection to your goals is the most important aspect of manifesting! In fact, researchers at Harvard University found that actually *seeing* something and then *imagining* that same thing activates the same parts of the brain. Dr. Donald Hilton also explained in 2014 that living an experience and visualizing it in your mind has the same effect.

Your mind can't tell whether something you're envisioning is real or not; therefore, you can take advantage of your biology and trick your brain into believing that you're already exactly where you want to be. This is why cultivating those winning emotions while you meditate, visualize, journal, or do any other mindful practice is fundamental for manifesting. It's not only about picturing that mental image in your mind. The magic lies in having a whole-body, holistic experience that convinces your brain you already have everything you desire.

Fill your days with things, people, and places that make you feel good. Give thanks often, do the things you love repeatedly, take sacred time for yourself every day, and fill your cup with all the positive energies you want to attract. When life gives you lemons, make lemonade!

Chapter 14:

Healing Your Inner Child

I first learned about inner child work through Ho'oponopono. Ho'oponopono is an ancient Hawaiian practice founded by Dr. Hew Len. He healed an entire ward of mental patients who had shown no signs of improvement without even visiting the ward in person. You can read more about this study online, but many of you may already know the magic that is Ho'oponopono. It consists of expressing, feeling, and repeating four phrases, the most powerful words someone can say:

I'm sorry.
Please forgive me.
Thank you.
I love you.

When you say these four powerful statements, you feel a deep and powerful healing. Remember, your healing journey spreads like wildfire and ignites the healing process of count-less others. The way the method works is, you say these four phrases and cleanse yourself of memories stored from your childhood and possibly memories you've stored from your ancestors of things they went through that were unconsciously passed down to you. Ancestral memories are often why some children have a seemingly random emerging phobia, of spiders for example, at a young age, despite having no prior exposure to the thing they're most afraid of. It's often a physical mani-festation of an ancestral memory passed down to them. Once the child learns how to heal that memory and remove it from their being, their life can transform quite dramatically.

The process above isn't only reserved for children, of course. Adults are fully capable of experiencing this phenome-non just as strongly. Once we bring the memories and traumas that we hold inside of us to the surface of our consciousness, we clear the path for some magnificently transformational shifts in our lives.

Tapping into my inner child when I was going through immense suffering and anxiety was certainly life-changing for me. I'd never connected the dots of the traumas I'd been through in my early childhood with the sabotaging behaviors that continued to play out in my romantic relationships. Push-ing my partners away and never feeling good enough for any man came down to me storing the trauma of when I was sex-ually abused in my teenage years. It never occurred to me that I hadn't healed that wound. For many years, I battled letting go of what I can only describe as one of the most terrifying experiences of my existence, then I realized you don't need to forget I; you only need to let go of it.

Forgiveness is completely different than forgetting, and with every new experience, we have a choice to make. Are we going to hold onto it and let it continue to sabotage our reality? Or do we choose to let it go and free ourselves of all attachment to that experience?

Healing my inner child was my ultimate cure, and I know it can help you too, whether you have a deep-rooted trauma you need to let go of or you feel overshadowed by limiting beliefs about money, love, health, or confidence. When you heal that energy inside of you, realizing that something greater than you is at play, you draw back the curtains and let in the light of your soul like a stream of sunlight through your window.

Let's visit our inner child together right now. Read this exercise through once or twice and then close your eyes and go through it if it feels right for you to do so.

I want you to imagine that standing before you is a younger version of yourself as a child. Imagine yourself at around six or seven years old. Take a moment to picture this. I want you to really look at yourself. Appreciate the innocent beauty of who you were as a child—a pure soul, full of love, light, and laughter, without any fears or doubts in sight, fully expressing and shining your light on the world. Would you ever tell that child that he or she isn't enough? That they were not worthy? Would you ever tell that little child that they were an idiot? Would you ever speak to them in the way that you sometimes speak to yourself? Correct me if I'm wrong, but I don't think you would ever condemn that little person to such maltreatment. You wouldn't fill that little version of you with anything other than unconditional love, right? So why do you do it to yourself?

Now, close your eyes, get comfortable in your seat with a straight spine, and put your hands on your heart (skin to skin is even better). Now, speak to your inner child. Take some deep breaths in through your nose and exhale loudly out through your mouth making a "ha" sound, allowing any heaviness to leave your body. Repeat this simple breathwork for a couple of minutes.

Recognize your connection with your inner child, the purest version of you. As you go deeper, be open and honest with your answers. Once you've connected, ask your inner child if they have any messages for you. They may not answer straight away. You may sense a hesitancy from them to show you that answer. Give them time. It may not come in the first, second, or even third repetition of this practice; for others, it may appear instantaneously. In the moments that follow, I want you to ask your inner child if you have hurt them in any way. As the answer comes up, don't react, just accept it, and listen. Be patient with yourself and give yourself the chance to open your heart to this.

Now, I want you to reach out a hand to your inner child and tell them, in dulcet tones, "I'm here for you now. I want to help you." Keep repeating these phrases until you feel the emotions rise within you: "I'm sorry I hurt you. I forgive myself fully. I forgive myself for making the same mistake twice. I'm sorry. Please forgive me. Please forgive me for hurting you and not listening to you. I promise to listen to you and honor you from now on."

Embrace them now. Wrap your arms around them and give them a hug right now. Hold them and repeat "thank you" four times. Make sure they know how grateful you are for their guidance. Finally, tell them how much you love and appreciate them: "I love you. I love you. I love you." It's normal for this to be emotional; it's a good thing. Outpouring of emotion signifies your release of pain and trauma through the method of Ho'oponopono. You're learning to heal your inner child. As you practice this more and more, your inner child will be there for you, and their guidance will become ever more apparent. When you hear that little intuitive voice within, when you feel those emotions rising from the core of your being, you must really listen. That is your inner child speaking to you.

This can be a profoundly life-changing experience. Upon fully healing, you'll find all those pains and traumas you've been through disintegrate into the ether. I'm not referring to forgetting them, just forgiving them and accepting that they do not define who you are now or the person you're becoming. You are destined to be something far greater than the bounds of your past experiences. But allow those experiences to continue to occupy a small space in your heart to remind you of the road less traveled you were willing to take to overcome your traumas and step into your destiny. Award yourself that privilege. You deserve it.

Conclusion

oming to the end of the winding road we've walked hand in hand through the pages of this book, I want to ask you the most important question of all. This time, knowing that there are no limitations in your mind, knowing that you are aware of how to create your reality from an abundant mindset, knowing that you can *absolutely* have it all . . . Who are you? Who will *you* inspire? Who and what do you represent? What are your values? Who do you *believe* you are? Who will you choose to show up as every day from this day forward?

Visualize your answer. Feel it in the deepest fibers of your being. Be that future self, right now and forever more. Be that happy, healthy being who has *already* hit their first million, who has a beautiful family to share their wealth with, who is making a positive impact in this world, who is repeatedly inspiring others, who has the means to help charities all around the world with causes that matter, who has achieved

171

and exceeded their biggest career goals. How does it feel to *be* that person you were always meant to become?

You *have* what it takes to **Be It Until You Become It.** The future *is* in your hands. You *are* the author of your own story, and from this point onward, you will direct the movie of your life and cast yourself in the role you wish to play in the game we call life. This is up to no one else, just you in co-creation with the Universe, reflecting your energy back to the collective consciousness.

Your future is yet to be written

So, what will you write?

Thank you for reading my book!

DOWNLOAD YOUR FREE GIFTS

Just to say thanks for buying and reading my book, I would like to give you a few free bonus gifts, no strings attached!

To download your free gifts, visit:
www.NatashaGraziano.com/Freegift

If you enjoyed reading this book and felt you gained value from it, it would mean the world to me if you would leave a review on your favorite bookstore website with your feedback, as this is how we make content and knowledge go viral. When we learn and share with the world, we're able to change so many more lives.

Thank you in advance.
You are always loved. I love you.
—Natasha.

About the Author

Natasha Graziano is ranked the "#1 Female Motivational Speaker under 40" as seen in *Forbes* magazine. Natasha helps people realize their full potential, activate it, and scale their message online.

From having written for Kourtney Kardashian's *Poosh* magazine, to appearing multiple times in the *New York Times*, Natasha coaches A listers as well as nine and ten figure entrepreneurs. With over 17 million followers on social media, it makes her one of the most influential thought leaders today.

From a homeless, broke, single mum in 2018, Natasha transformed her life and is now a *Best Selling* author who speaks on stages and at events alongside the likes of Gary

Vaynerchuk, Tai Lopez, Grant Cardone, Tony Robbins, Mark Cuban, to name just a few.

Natasha is the host of *The Law of Attraction* podcast which has had over 100 million views and is often ranked in the top three podcasts on Apple's Top Shows for Education.

Endnotes

1   Luc LaMontagne, "The Neural Correlates of the Subconscious," Mind 4 (Fall 2020): 3–7.

2   Ernest S. Holmes, The Science of Mind (United States: Pacific Publishing Studio, 2011), 97.

3   The National Academies of Science, Engineering, and Medicine, "Child Development and Early Learning: A Foundation for Professional Knowledge and Competencies," https://nap.nationalacademies.org/resource/19401/ProfKnowCompFINAL.pdf.

4   The National Academies of Science, Engineering, and Medicine, "Child Development and Early Learning: A Foundation for Professional Knowledge and Competencies," https://nap.nationalacademies.org/resource/19401/ProfKnowCompFINAL.pdf.

5   Dr. William D. Horton, "What is the RAS?" https://drwillhorton.com/ras/.

6   John C. Maxwell, The 15 Invaluable Laws of Growth (New York: Hachette Book Group, 2012).

7   Dr. Nina Radcliff, "Resentment and its impact on your health" (Press of Atlantic City, March 28, 2021), https:// pressofatlanticcity.com/lifestyles/health-med-fit/resentment -and-its-impact-on-your-health-dr-nina-radcliff/article_ 9f4eaca4-e1a9-5ee1-ac52-b38cd20c6cbc.html.

8   Joseph Murphy, The Power of Your Subconscious Mind (Mansfield Centre, CT: Martino Publishing, 2011).

9   Wei-Jie Wu et al, "Morning breathing exercises prolong lifespan by improving hyperventilation in people living with respiratory cancer," Medicine 96, no. 2 (January 2017), doi: 10.1097/MD.0000000000005838.

10 King's College London, "Do negative thoughts increase risk of Alzheimer's disease?" November 17, 2014, https:// medicalxpress.com/news/2014-11-negative-thoughts- alzheimer-disease.html.

11 Michael D. Robinson & Rebecca J. Compton, "The happy mind in action: The cognitive basis of subjective well-being." In The Science of Subjective Well-being, ed. M. Eid & R. J. Larsen (Guilford Press, 2008), 220–238.

12 E.A. Locke, K.N. Shaw, L.M. Saari, & G.P. Latham, "Goal setting and task performance: 1969–1980," Psychological Bulletin, 90, no. 1 (1981), 125–152. https:// doi.org/10.1037/0033-2909.90.1.125.

13 Rollin McCraty & Maria A. Zayas, "Cardiac coherence, self-regulation, autonomic stability, and psychosocial well-being," Frontiers in Psychology 5, no. 1090 (September 29, 2014), doi:10.3389/fpsyg.2014.01090.

14 Joseph Murphy, The Power of Your Subconscious Mind (Mansfield Centre, CT: Martino Publishing, 2011).

15 Wallace D. Wattles, The Science of Getting Rich (Createspace Independent Publishing, 2018).

16 Joseph Murphy, The Power of Your Subconscious Mind (Mansfield Centre, CT: Martino Publishing, 2011).

17 World Health Organization, "Healthy diet," https://www. who.int/initiatives/behealthy/healthy-diet.

18 Matthew Walker, "Science of Better Sleep," MasterClass, https://www.masterclass.com/classes/matthew-walker-teaches-the-science-of-better-sleep.

19 Matthew Walker, "Science of Better Sleep," MasterClass, https://www.masterclass.com/classes/matthew-walker-teaches-the-science-of-better-sleep.

20 Napoleon Hill, Think and Grow Rich (Shippensburg, PA: Sound Wisdom, 1937).

21 Joseph Murphy, The Power of Your Subconscious Mind (Mansfield Centre, CT: Martino Publishing, 2011).

22 Brendan McCaughey, "The Power of Words," Medium, December 26, 2018, https://multitude27.medium.com/the-power-of-words-61c524ddf1b5.

23 William Powers, "Law of Detachment," William Powers Books, September 10, 2015, https://williampowersbooks.com/2015/09/law-of-detachment/.

24 Christopher Myers, "What's Positive about Failure?" Michigan Ross Center for Positive Organizations, Uni-

versity of Michigan, March 28, 2014, https://positiveorgs.
bus.umich.edu/news/whats-positive-about-failure/.

25 Christopher Myers, "What's Positive about Failure?"
Michigan Ross Center for Positive Organizations, University of Michigan, March 28, 2014, https://positiveorgs.
bus.umich.edu/news/whats-positive-about-failure/.

26 Team Tony, "6 TIPS TO LEAVE YOUR COMFORT
ZONE," Tony Robbins, https://www.tonyrobbins.com/
productivity-performance/leave-comfort-zone/.

27 Brainworks, "WHAT ARE BRAINWAVES?" https://
brainworksneurotherapy.com/what-are-brainwaves.

28 Zuzana Koudelková & Martin Strmiska, "Introduction
to the identification of brain waves based on their frequency," MATEC Web of Conferences, 2018.

A free ebook edition is available with the purchase of this book.

To claim your free ebook edition:

1. Visit MorganJamesBOGO.com
2. Sign your name CLEARLY in the space
3. Complete the form and submit a photo of the entire copyright page
4. You or your friend can download the ebook to your preferred device

Morgan James BOGO™

A **FREE** ebook edition is available for you or a friend with the purchase of this print book.

CLEARLY SIGN YOUR NAME ABOVE

Instructions to claim your free ebook edition:
1. Visit MorganJamesBOGO.com
2. Sign your name CLEARLY in the space above
3. Complete the form and submit a photo of this entire page
4. You or your friend can download the ebook to your preferred device

Print & Digital Together Forever.

Snap a photo

Free ebook

Read anywhere